THE POLITICS OF CHANGE
A Jamaican Testament

THE POLITICS
OF CHANGE

A Jamaican Testament

MICHAEL MANLEY

ANDRE DEUTSCH

First published 1974 by
André Deutsch Limited
105 Great Russell Street London WC1

Printed in Great Britain by
Tonbridge Printers Ltd
Tonbridge, Kent

Hardback edition ISBN 0 233 96504 1
Paperback edition ISBN 0 233 96519 x

To Beverley

Contents

'Freedom is the expression of the creative in life. It is neither an inherent right nor a hard-won value. It is a law of being, lacking which there would be no evolution, no progress, no civilization, only primal chaos set in permanence.'

NORMAN W. MANLEY.

'Chance has never yet satisfied the hope of a suffering people. Action, self-reliance, the vision of self and the future have been the only means by which the oppressed have seen and realized the light of their own freedom.'

MARCUS GARVEY.

Preface

THIS book is written with two not unrelated objectives in mind. After twenty-one years in the public life of Jamaica as a journalist, trade unionist and politician, I felt the need to clarify, in my own mind, the effect of this activist involvement upon the ideals and principles which I brought to the enterprise in the first place.

At the same time, it seemed to me that there was need to reconsider and restate, from the standpoint of the 1970s, a philosophical road which Jamaica might explore as an independent nation.

The anarchists, the racialists and the extremists of the radical left and intransigent right have offered labels interspersed with fragments of advice. These prescriptions, however, have added up to something rather less than a viable strategy.

I hope that this book may serve as a point of departure for the realistic discussion of Jamaica's future; her possibilities and problems; her strengths and weaknesses; most importantly the hopes she may dare to entertain and the ideals to which she should be committed; the dream, the vision of justice against which she must measure her shortcomings.

I do not attempt to specify a plan of action nor a quantitative analysis of our problems. Neither do I presume to articulate a new political philosophy. Rather, I seek to remind my reader that a number of categories in the political dialogue have real meaning and summon us to both commitment and action. The notions of equality, social justice and self-reliance are, accordingly, invoked as reminders of human purpose.

Hopefully, this book will be of interest to people in all developing countries, indeed to all who are concerned with politics and the human condition. It is of course written by a Jamaican for Jamaicans and by a working politician for people who must, every day, seek to make some sense of lives beset by difficulties which are as pressing as they must seem incomprehensible.

My gratitude goes first of all to my wife who gave me the courage to try; and for her patience and unflagging interest; to Doctor, the Right Honourable Eric Williams, Prime Minister of Trinidad and Tobago, who encouraged me with the supreme compliment of thinking I might have something worthwhile to say, and, also in this regard, to my lifelong friend, the author, Mr John Hearne; to Mr Rex Nettleford of the University of the West Indies for his help with editing, structuring and the ordering of ideas alike; to Mr Alister McIntyre, also of the University of the West Indies, for his constructive criticism and many useful suggestions; to Mrs Corina Meeks for a close reading which yielded much of benefit; to Mrs Barbara Mowatt who, helped by Mrs Carmen Gauntlett, Mrs Linda Schmitt and Mrs Ena Keating from time to time, bore the brunt of the typing with unfailing good nature and much skill; to my publisher, Mr André Deutsch, for a transatlantic correspondence which bolstered my spirits when they seemed to flag; and finally to all the others, too numerous to mention, who have helped in so many ways.

Of course, gratitude is not enough for my mother and late father whose efforts separately and together contributed so much to the processes of transformation which we must now seek to continue.

M. M.
Jamaica. April 1973.

PART I

A Philosophy of Change

Introduction

ALL organized societies depend on a power system; and politics is the business of power, its acquisition and its use. Observation of history suggests that there have been three approaches to politics and, therefore, three approaches to the use of power. There are men, perhaps the majority, who see power as something to be acquired for its own sake. Then there are those who see power as something to be used for purposes of minor adjustments in the society. Finally, there are the idealists who seek to arrange fundamental change.

In the first case, men who pursue power for its own sake usually do so, either because it satisfies something in their own egotism or because they want for themselves the fruits of power; and of course, it is in this stream that the great tyrants of history are to be found.

The second group does not necessarily want power for its own sake so much as for the achievement of some immediate adjustment in the society. It sees society as an amoral phenomenon to be accepted in all fundamental respects and adjusted in terms of obvious points of inefficiency or in response to the particular pressures of discontent. Throughout history these have been broadly grouped in the great conservative parties such as the Conservative Party of Great Britain; the conservative wings of both the Democratic and Republican Parties of the USA; the Christian Democratic Party of Germany and so on. In all these parties it will be observed that the people who lead them begin with the assumption that their existing social framework is sound and reasonable; but more importantly, just 'is' in the sense that it exists. Thus, beginning with a complete acceptance of the *status quo*, society is viewed in an essentially superficial way and the question then asked: 'How can it be made a little more efficient?' This type of politician is conscious of points of pressure, seeming to require change, that arise from discontent and seeks, in response to that pressure, marginal adjustments in the organization of society for the purpose of relieving the discontent and removing the points of pressure.

Finally, there are the idealists who begin by rejecting existing social relationships and proceed to construct a model of how they think society should be ordered. They are concerned with the basic changes that are necessary to effect the transformation from the one state to the other.

Our second group are the pragmatists of political history. They probably spend more time in power than any other kind of politician because, obviously, societies discover in the end that tyrants exercise power at the expense of everybody else. So our first category is liable to sudden and violent elimination.

On the other hand, idealists, the third category, are vulnerable because they are concerned with change. Change and oppression both breed fear, and therefore, the pragmatic politician who is content to tinker is the one with whom societies feel most comfortable. Tyranny, as a method, has no place in this book. On the other hand, Jamaican society is disfigured by inequities that go too deep for tinkering. Our concern, therefore, must be with the politics of change.

Idealistic politicians seek first a moral foundation for political action. At different points of history, different issues seem of preponderant significance and, therefore, lead to different emphases in the search for a moral frame. But at the root of all idealistic political thinking is the question: What is the purpose of political organization? Some answer this with the notion of stability. Taking, therefore, stability as the first order of priorities, a theoretical social system is constructed with order as its main objective. Others take the contrary view and see individual freedom as their first order of priorities. With equal devotion these will construct a system that seeks to reverse every priority of the first category. Where the first will make obedience, conformity and 'law and order' the dominant consideration, the second group will seek a system that minimises these considerations and prefers rather to walk as close to the edge of anarchy as social survival will allow.

More recently, the dialogue has shifted from questions of authority and liberty to the more apparently relevant consideration of wealth. And so most contemporary political idealism has

centred on the question of the distribution of wealth within a
society. In the last hundred years, this question has dominated
the political dialogue and has produced political philosophies
claiming allegiance to capitalism with its emphasis on notions
of liberty and the creation of wealth; and to communism, which
has evolved into the idea that the equitable distribution of wealth
can only be ensured within the frame of an authoritarian system.

In all this, the Socialist, so called, has sought to resolve the
paradox by suggesting that a libertarian democratic system can
provide the matrix within which wealth is distributed and individual liberty preserved.

Like all political leaders who belong to the idealistic stream,
broadly defined, I have found myself constantly in the presence
of a personal, moral imperative: How to isolate a single, central
thesis of belief from the welter of conflicting moral categories. Of
course, one must be concerned with equitable distribution of
wealth, with social stability and order, with individual liberty.
But always the suggestion has lurked that these categories are in
conflict and that the political idealist must make a choice. I reject
this notion. The more that I have thought about the morality of
politics, the more there has emerged for me a single touchstone
of right and wrong; and the touchstone is to be found in the
notion of equality.

Basically, society is a group of people pursuing the common
objective of survival. Stripped of all rhetorical excess, this is the
point at which social organization begins. However, even at the
survival level, this implies the survival of every individual; and if
we accept that everybody is entitled to survive, then we have
conceded the foundation of the notion of equality. Later, societies
can expand the notion of survival to include the category of
progress. By this I mean, not merely eating enough to keep alive
for tomorrow's tasks. One may plan further ahead and wish to
put aside enough for next year's drought. In due course, having
provided for next year's drought, one may wish to produce
enough in six days to be able to enjoy a day of rest. In due
course, one wants to be able to produce enough in forty-eight
working weeks of five days to be able to rest two days a week
and four weeks a year. In due course, one will be concerned with
producing enough to have a real opportunity of creative activity
within the two days of rest and the four weeks of vacation. And

at no point can one logically abandon the notion that everybody is seeking the two days of rest and the four weeks of vacation and the ability to enjoy them. The more I have thought, therefore, about social organization, the more I have concluded that here is only one supreme, moral imperative that cannot be affected by time, by circumstance, by the seasons, by man's moods or intellectual distractions, by the injunctions of philosophers or the sermons of pastors; and it is the notion that social organization exists to serve everybody or it has no moral foundation.

At this point, one has to be clear that the notion of equality in society does not imply either that everybody possesses equal talents or interests, or capabilities; nor that everybody ought to receive the same reward for the function they perform. Obviously, it is of the essence of the human condition that the variations of human personality are infinite. Equally, the fact of specialization within the social organization implies a difference of function, which, in turn, leads to differing rewards. But the fact that society cannot function effectively without differentials in rewards together with the fact that men are manifestly not equal in talent must not be allowed to obscure the central purpose of social organization. This is, and must always be, the promotion of the welfare of every member of the human race. The moment that this intellectual distinction is understood, the concept of equality becomes clear and free from confusions that arise from other aspects of the social mechanism. If you begin with the notion of equality, all the other moral considerations in social organization take their place. Authority ceases to be an aim in itself and becomes merely the pre-condition of the survival of the whole group. Individual liberty ceases to be a petulant distraction and becomes the extent to which all men may pursue their creative potential within the framework of social survival. And to the extent that the requirements of survival conflict with the thrust for individual expression, the notion of equality provides a frame of reference within which a solution may be found.

It will be the purpose of this book to examine the condition of a newly independent society encumbered with the economic, social and psychological consequences of three hundred years of colonialism and to see how far the notion of equality can supply the key to an economic, social, political – indeed, a national strategy.

I

The Setting for Change

IN the early post-colonial phase of a developing country, only political movements devoted to the politics of change have relevance. An analysis of the legacies of colonialism suggests a degree of social debilitation together with economic and social malformations so grave as to make the politics of tinkering within the *status quo,* irrelevant to our condition.

Let us, therefore, turn to a consideration of some of the broad characteristics that are common to most post-colonial societies and that are all the more evident the longer the particular exposure to the colonial experience.

Jamaica is a classic example of this situation because its history involved being born in the colonial condition followed by three hundred years of unbroken experience in that milieu before it finally attained its political independence.

A mere 4,000 odd square miles, 144 miles long, with mountains soaring to more than 7,000 feet, Jamaica is an interesting mixture of challenge and opportunity. Its fertile plains boast first-class soil and are ideal for intensive agriculture. Much of the island is mountainous, however, and poses for the farmer the special problem of sloping terrain. Its bauxite deposits are among the largest in the world. Its beaches are a standing invitation to the vacationer and its interior often breathtakingly beautiful. Its two million people are ninety per cent black, the descendants of slaves and most of the rest coloured. There are very few unmixed survivors of the former white slave-owning planters.

The plains are still devoted to sugar cane cultivation. The hills support a small farmer population that traces its origins back to first escaped and, later, freed slaves who sought to rest their new-found freedom upon the economic foundation of bits of land that were their own. This, then, is the land that was born to the colonial experience when the British captured it from the Spanish in 1655 and that knew no other political experience for three hundred and seven years: surely one of the longest, unbroken periods of colonial rule in modern history.

Jamaica was the meeting place of two expatriate populations: the Britisher uprooting himself in search of quick wealth through sugar; and the African uprooted by force from his environment to supply the slave labour upon which his owner's dream of wealth depended. Two uprooted populations, the one adapting its own culture to a new environment and the other subjected to pressures designed to obliterate all cultural recollection, confronted each other in Jamaica and provided through their common experience a unique variant on the colonial theme. This is so because all colonialism involves a process of cultural displacement. Where, however, the subject people are conquered on their home ground, a measure of cultural continuity is preserved. At least, it may be presumed that cultural confidence will reflect an element of indigenous survival. Jamaican, indeed Caribbean, experience has this significant difference, however, in that the African slave was torn from his family, transported across an ocean and there assiduously prevented from forming new family groups which could pass on the remembered culture of the homeland. It is in this cultural vacuum that colonialism held unbroken sway for three centuries.

Much has been written of the economic consequences of colonialism, but it might be as well to remind ourselves briefly that colonial economies were conceived in the context of dependence. The purpose of a colonial economy was to produce primary products for the metropolitan power and to provide a market for the more sophisticated range of consumer goods which were the economic preserve of the metropolitan power. The wealth that was created was in the main repatriated to the 'Mother Country' and provided one of the primary engines in the capital accumulation process which marked the industrial revolution in the eighteenth and nineteenth centuries.

Since the colony was seen as existing only to serve metropolitan needs, the use of slave labour was a natural extension of the system which, as is the case with all empires, found its rationale in the conscious assumption of the superior moral and historical destiny of the colonizing people. The end product of this system was a colonial economy consisting of three main elements: the productive sector of the economy was geared to supply primary agricultural products, the labour force was in the main controlled to supply the cheap labour needed to plant and reap these products; and the rest of the economy consisted of traders whose sole purpose was the importation of the entire range of consumer goods required by the population. To this one could add, in Jamaica's case, a peasant farmer structure and a cadre of professional and vocational people providing basic services such as health, education and the like.

This economic pattern is so well documented and has been so accurately analysed and exhaustively discussed that it has often obscured a deeper consequence of colonialism which, not understood, can reduce to impotence the most skilfully devised plan for reshaping the very economic pattern which I have just summarized. I refer here to the psychology of dependence which is the most insidious, elusive and intractable of the problems which we inherit.

If a man is denied both responsibility and power long enough he will lose the ability to respond to the challenge of the first and to grasp the opportunity of the second. One has only to look at what happens to the youth of the ghetto if they fail to find a job over a number of years. The time comes when they become incapable of performing inside that complex framework of disciplines that make up the average working situation. So too with societies; denied responsibility and power long enough, they show a similar tendency and can become almost incapable of response to opportunity because there is not the habit of self-reliance.

If one scans the horizon of the Jamaican experience in, say, 1962, at the moment of our independence, (Jamaica became independent on 6th August, 1962) one has only to select areas at random to see the insidious, pervasive effect of the colonial experience. Neither did the heroic call to racial pride of a Marcus Garvey; nor the momentous march to independence under Norman Manley; nor even the collective experience of self-discipline of the modern Trade Union Movement launched by Alexander Bustamante, Florizel Glasspole and Ken Hill, together with the political party system, make more than a dent upon the problem.

Take, for example, our educational system. It was imported lock, stock and barrel from England without a moment's thought about its relevance to Jamaica's needs and aspirations. This was not because of a failure of the intellect on the part of those who transplanted it. Rather, I suggest that there was a failure of perception: an inability to perceive that the first responsibility of the educator is to address his mind – *his* mind, not somebody else's mind – to the question of *our* needs. In a very profound sense this calls for an almost traumatic process of release from the psychology of dependence. It is a trauma that we are only now, in 1972, beginning to face as the necessary precursor to the development of an educational system of our own.

Take again, the attitude of the average community in Jamaica. The basic instinct of the majority of the members of any community precludes the chance that they ask themselves the question: 'What do *we* need and what can we do to provide it for *ourselves*?' – adding as a necessary afterthought: 'Let us see what we need from government to bridge the gap between what *we* can do and the totality of *our* needs.' On the contrary, the question is phrased the other way around: 'How much can we get the *government* to provide of what we need now?' They will add, as an after-thought, 'I suppose we will have to wait until some unspecified point of time in the future for the difference between what government can do now and the totality of our needs to be met by the government.' Again, the whole question of psychological dependence lies at the root of the distinction between these two attitudes.

Consider finally, the Trade Union Movement. Critics have constantly inveighed against the tendency of the Jamaica Trade Union Movement to reply upon middle class leadership. The criticism is well-directed, but the nature of the problem is misconceived. At the root of the psychology of the Trade Union Movement in Jamaica, is not, as one might expect, the self-reliance that is normally inherent in the institution itself. Instead we find the same psychology of dependence which tends to seek in this case, not a government, but a leader who is expected to bear the brunt of the decision-making process. Obviously, where individual authority is substituted for collective responsibility, the better-educated man is more likely to be able to cope with the situation and produce solutions. Again, the critical question is: 'Why is there this tendency to assume that responsibility does not reside in *me*, in my own situation, but in some external authority which I will invest with authority for the translation of my dreams into reality?'

Later on we will attempt to deal specifically with colonial attitudes in the wider sense and this will involve the exploration of attitudes to work. But for the moment, it is enough to make the broad assertion that the first task that a post-colonial society must tackle is the development of a strategy designed to replace the psychology of dependence with the spirit of individual and collective self-reliance. Until that exercise is successfully embarked upon every other plan will fail. Indeed, without the spirit of self-reliance, it is doubtful if a successful indigenous plan can be devised; instead time and energy may be dissipated in the adaptation of other people's plans, designed for other situations, to solve other people's problems.

When one considers the magnitude of the economic and attitudinal restructuring which our condition demands, it becomes clear that the politics of conservatism and tinkering are not only irrelevant to our situation but represent an intolerable default of responsibility. *Man can adjust by tinkering but he cannot transform.* Nothing less than transformation can provide answers to the dilemmas within which we are currently trapped.

2

Multi-Party Politics and Change

SINCE politics is about the organization of power, and political systems the method of organization employed, the whole subject of political method is best approached in terms of preferences rather than absolutes and more safely discussed in the language of analysis than dogma. I think that one must begin by keeping clearly in mind two completely unrelated phenomena each of which has a profound bearing on the question of political systems. First, there is the question of the natural sociological tendency of a particular people at a particular point in time; and secondly, there is the question of objectives.

Let us consider what we mean by 'natural sociological tendency'. At any moment of history a social group will reflect a sum total of historical experience. This experience accumulates through the generations and is handed down by father to son, in writings, in speeches which leave their impression upon audiences and eventually adds up to a complex pattern of habits. It is this 'pattern of habits' which I describe as the 'natural sociological tendency'. For example, if we take the Russia which Lenin inherited by the route of revolution, we find a society that had become historically accustomed to three traditions. First, there was the tradition of absolute rule which can be traced through Ivan the Terrible, Peter the Great, Catherine and so on, down to the final disaster of the last Nicholas. Second, there was the elitist tradition with an established aristocracy which supplied the officer corps of successive armies, among other things; and finally, there was the tradition of feudal subservience. Against this background, it is perhaps not surprising that the political method adopted by the revolution bore a striking resemblance to all that had gone before. Stalin was to a remarkable degree in the tradition of the great Czars even to the extent of the paranoiac excesses which he shared with Ivan. It is noticeable that the Communist Party of Russia was, and remains, organized on the basis of a tight elitist cadre which wields absolute political power over every aspect of Russian life. And finally, one must notice that the acceptance of this high degree of centralized power by the people at large presents a striking parallel to centuries of earlier experience. Of course, one understands that the objectives of czarist rule and the communist regime are totally different. But the methods are similar and prompt the enquiry: was the method of modern, communist Russia a completely free, rational and morally motivated choice amongst alternatives; or did it reflect an insight, on the part of the leaders of the revolution, into the method most likely to succeed because of an historically induced 'natural tendency' of the Russian people?

We can now move to another continent and consider the tendency in post-colonial Africa to move towards the one-party state model. Western metropolitan horror in the face of this spectacle is misplaced. Modern Africa south of the Sahara comes to independence against the background of its own experience which, in spite of the brief intervention of colonialism, is tribal. At the heart of the tribal instinct is the assumption that the social group is one and indivisible. Also to be found in this experience are the role of the chief and an acceptance of the process of group discussion. Nowhere, however, is there a place in the historical experience for the idea of the systematic division of the group into opposing camps. The fact that this was a feature of political organization in some colonising powers is hardly likely to commend itself to people who associate their imperial masters with exploitation. While more than prepared to absorb the superior technology of their former masters, Africans probably associated their political methods with the business of external rule and exploitation. Against this background, it is surely not surprising that African nations do not take naturally at this stage of their evolution to the idea of parliamentary democracy based on the Westminster model which is predicated upon the idea of contained conflict between contending groups. After all, if conflict within containment is necessary to the system, who is to be responsible for the containment and what is the background of experience that leads a people to contain themselves as part of a pattern of instinctive conduct?

In this situation, it is fascinating to observe how the problem has been approached by the greatest contemporary African political thinker, Julius Nyerere. Beginning with the thesis that society is not different from the tribe and that both represent an extension of the family, Nyerere has sought to construct a genuinely democratic model that is consistent with the logic of Africa's situation. The Nyerere model involves a one-party state which is a logical extension of the 'natural tendency' of the Tanzanian people. However, he has sought to build into a one-party state a genuine democracy, in the sense of a political system that is founded in the notion of dialogue, discussion, debate, dissent, respect for minorities and minority opinions and resting upon genuinely free elections in which particular representatives are subject to recall through the elective process. There is no contemporary political model which reflects more completely an attempt to marry the ancient and eternal ideal of democracy in the sense of government by the people with the 'natural tendency' of a people, than the Nyerere model. Indeed it is the consideration of this model which, more than any other, prompts me to the earlier caution that political systems are better approached in terms of analysis than dogma.

Let us now turn to the question of objectives and then see if we can come back to some point at which tendency and objective may be synthesised in an approach that is relevant to a country like Jamaica. By 'objective' I mean: What does a person addressing his mind to the question of politics seek to achieve in terms of social and economic result, as a consequence of the employment of a political method? If the primary objective is power for its own sake, then the method will be despotic. If the primary objective is the maintenance of the *status quo*, then the method adopted will vary in accordance with whether the system now in force is achieving the end or not. For example, if a two-party democracy has created such a fine balance between parties, as to render effective change almost impossible of accomplishment, the defenders of the *status quo* will obviously be content with the political methods that are achieving that end. If, on the other hand, a group of idealists seek to mobilize rapid change, they may opt for a one-party state and an essentially totalitarian method as an expression of their own impatience and because that is the method most likely to allow for rapid change by compulsion rather than gradual change by persuasion. Equally, another group of idealists may feel that the rulers in a totalitarian political system are using the control of power to prevent change, in which case our group will have to oust the rulers. Thereafter they must either rest with the capture of the totalitarian machine on the one hand, or plan to effect the substitution of a genuinely democratic political method, on the other.

The permutations and combinations inherent in the situation are infinite. The challenge and opportunity of Third World political development is to be found in this sheer range of choice. Equally, the question of what is capable of accomplishment will be profoundly influenced by the 'natural tendency', as we have just defined it, of the people concerned.

Against this background, let us consider the question of a society which needs to be changed, whose leadership is committed to equality and whose traditional method is democratic. Such a society is to be found in Jamaica. Now, why do we say that Jamaica needs to be changed? Obviously, any society in which one quarter of the adult population cannot read or write, in which one quarter of the total work force has no job and in which the distribution of the ownership of land and of the means of production represent gross and growing inequalities, is an affront to any notion of social justice, however loosely defined.

There are many people looking at the need for change in Jamaica who have questioned whether the democratic process can supply the framework within which this can be achieved. A one-party state is proposed as an alternative. The argument is attractive because it seems to hold out the promise of quick results. The protagonists of a one-party system for Jamaica argue that our present two-party habit makes it difficult to mobilise acceptance for change in the society and leads to a constant division of the national will. Indeed, they go further and argue that a two-party system is in duty bound to fracture the national will, because of the established notion that 'it is the duty of the opposition to oppose'.

Superficially, the argument is logically persuasive, but, I suspect, owes more to the impatience of its spokesmen than to an understanding of Jamaican society. In considering alternatives for Jamaica, one must begin with an understanding of 'the natural tendency'. There is no question that the 'natural tendency' of the Jamaican people is individualistic, disputatious almost to the point of destructiveness, but rooted in a great, historically acquired strength: the ability to accept that the vote is the natural end product of dispute and that a majority decision is conclusive of an issue.

It is important to consider some of the historical factors which have operated to make this so. First of all, one must bear in mind the effect of slavery upon people who, when still in Africa, were part of social systems that depended on the acceptance of clear patterns of tribal and family discipline. This is an important factor in considering the development of modern African political institutions. In Jamaica's case, however, those who managed the institution of slavery set out deliberately to destroy all the social patterns which the original slaves brought with them. This was part of a conscious attempt to make the slave manageable by destroying in his own mind the sense of belonging to a cultural and social system which had intrinsic worth and which would, therefore, be worth fighting for. By the time of the abolition of slavery it is safe to say that these policies had worked to the extent that a human being had evolved with new attitudes reflecting new needs and in whom the old attitudes and values had in large measure ceased to be major determinants of behaviour.

Emerging from a background of sustained and total tyranny, it was inevitable that Jamaicans should enter the new condition of legal freedom with a profound distrust of authority which was, inevitably, associated with tyranny in the mind of every newly freed slave. This pattern is reflected in the great movements which took place leading to the establishment of the small farming settlements all over the mountains of Jamaica as men put the fact of physical distance between themselves and the former scenes of slavery in the sugar plains. In the case of those who remained to work on the sugar estates because of the pressures of economic reality, there was no noticeable resistance to the authority of the sugar owner because there were no economic alternatives available and because the newly freed worker had not yet learnt to create new institutions through which he could express his needs and gain confidence in his manhood. In short, the sugar worker bowed to plantation authority because he thought he had no choice. But there remained, nonetheless, the lingering resistance to the idea of authority as such. This expressed itself in opposition to any form of regimentation and in resentment of discipline. In this, the Jamaican shares a common experience with his brothers throughout the Caribbean, and indeed with all people whose present attitudes reflect a collective recollection of tyranny.

There is a clear parallel with British attitudes towards authority as they are expressed in political patterns since much of English history is the story of the resistance by groups in the society to the improper exercise of power by other groups. This is equally true of Europe and of course is fundamental to the American concept of political organization. Indeed, the American system is so dominated by the fear of tyranny as to have created political institutions that are almost unmanageable. American government is not designed so much to create the conditions for the effective exercise of authority as to make the exercise of authority subject to constant checks and balances. It is both notorious and tragic that this objective, which is achieved by the separation of powers under its constitution, often reduces the United States of America to the verge of paralysis in the face of the great problems of modern government. Its significance here is the extent to which it demonstrates the effect upon political institutions when these are designed by men in the shadow of the fear of tyranny. In Jamaica's case this fear is real and deep and creates the fundamental attitudinal climate within which the Jamaican approaches the question of his political institutions. Slavery has done for the Jamaican what monarchical and religious tyranny did for the American; and what the feudal barons, the landed aristocracy and finally, the new entrepreneurial rulers of the industrial revolution all combined to do for the Englishman.

To the Jamaican's historical distrust of authority must be added the fact that all the institutions through which the newly freed slave, and indeed the entire society, began to attain social coherence, were designed in the shadow of the Westminster model of democracy. Where, for example, African tribes may have been conquered in the late nineteenth century and endured a brief colonial interregnum spanning two or three generations at most, the Jamaican and Caribbean experience stretches back over centuries. In the century from 1838 to the modern revolution which began in 1938, the Baptist Church meetings and building societies and all the similar social responses to 'felt need' were organized by men who took parliamentary democracy as their model. Hence, the positive historical influences tended in the direction of Western style democracy and operated upon people who were acutely aware of tyranny and were, as a consequence, all too prone to suspect a permanent connection between authority and oppression. If we added to this the fact that the colonial system subsequent to the abolition of slavery continued to be oppressive in all respects other than the legal question of status that was involved in slavery, it can be seen that there was no new experience tending to present authority in a new light. So far from appearing to be the source of security and order in society, authority continued to be the instrument of oppression.

Against this background, therefore, one can readily see that there is something in the totality of the Jamaican's experience that makes him take naturally to any process which rests upon the containment of authority. This is partly a consequence of all that we have learned during the colonial experience; partly a product of building society meetings stretching back for over a hundred years in which men learned to sit down and debate and argue and take a vote to decide; partly the consequence of the influence of the Church, and partly the interaction of all these things upon each other.

Together they have fashioned a people who take naturally to argument and the solution of a problem by vote. Anybody who has lived through the trade union experience for example, knows that it is instinct in the Jamaican personality to argue, to be disputatious, to listen to contending views and eventually to say 'let us take a vote', or as the worker would put it: 'majority must carry'. Others formulate it as: 'majority must rule'. And to understand a people it is best to listen and discover what comes naturally to them. The democratic process comes naturally to the Jamaican people. Therefore, arguments about one-party states as against multi-party states begin with the supreme disadvantage of irrelevance in the Jamaican situation, because the one-party state is unthinkable to the Jamaican. And this is not because there cannot be democratic process within a one-party state. As Nyerere has demonstrated, this can be organized. However, such a system depends on the acceptance of the state and the government as representing a whole which cannot be opposed in an organized way. In the Westminster democratic model, state and government are conceived in more separate terms and it is entirely legitimate to organize opposition to the government. Where the historical experience reflects a profound sense of oppression, it is natural that the Westminster model should more readily accommodate the psychological needs of a people.

It is hardly a matter of coincidence, therefore, that as a Jamaican, I happen to prefer the democratic method. I prefer it because when I feed the question of political method into the equation of equality, it seems to me that the democratic method is more likely to afford an opportunity for equality than any totalitarian system yet devised. Starting with the touchstone of equality, the argument proceeds as follows: if the individual is to be equal in society, we must understand everything that equality implies. It implies access to a home, it implies access to a job. It implies access to the educational process and to remedy under the law. It implies access to leisure. It implies access to the accumulated creative experience of mankind. Above all, it implies a society that evokes from a man a sense of responsibility to his fellows.

If we really stop and analyze the social condition, it must imply all these things and it must imply both opportunity and that responsibility which is the other side of the coin of opportunity. We are talking, then, of men in the fullest sense of their capabilities. Man needs material security because he has physical needs. But he also has a creative side which is expressed in the arts, the world of ideas and in his scientific inventiveness. Access to homes, jobs, education, leisure, legal remedy are all capable of attainment in a one-party state, though not necessarily more rapidly than in a political system which permits organized dissent. However, there remains the question of dissent itself which is fundamental to the democratic process. This can be afforded a certain scope in a one-party state through careful planning of the system. The right of dissent, however, is most secure where the system contemplates the right of dissenters to organize separately. Now the right to dissent is the foundation of liberty and liberty is the climate within which man's creativity flourishes best.

Therefore, I prefer the method more likely to provide a continuing climate of freedom and to address my mind to the problem of ensuring that this method is also made to provide for man's material needs. Thus, to my mind, the democratic system which places a proper emphasis on the libertarian spirit is the political method which, wisely handled, is most likely to supply the context within which men can achieve the best that is in themselves.

Furthermore, if a society begins by natural tendency with the capacity to accept dissent as natural to politics, it would be a rape of history to seek to wrest it from that path and embark upon some other course that excludes from the system the surest guarantee of individual freedom.

Therefore, I repudiate the impatience for change with which we seek to undo and dismantle our present political strength and substitute for it some other system which would have to be artificially contrived to give effect to the purposes of impatience.

It is necessary to analyze some of the special problems that the democratic process poses for a developing society. This, in turn, must flow from a comprehension of the priorities of a developing society. Simply put, developing countries face the supreme problem of rapid transformation. At another time in history it was possible for societies to grow in terms of a quiet, continuing response to pressures that were peculiar to themselves, that were almost intimate in the sense of their being separated from external influence. Modern technology, however, has created a world in which philosophy communicates itself instantly around the globe. The philosophy of equality translates to the average man into simple practical aspirations. These aspirations are of necessity material at first. This has meant that everywhere in the world there is now a simultaneous demand for access to goods and services comparable with those available to the most advanced societies in the world. But the accomplishment of this objective involves internal and external strategies which for young, developing nations are of enormous difficulty and complexity.

At the heart of the question of internal strategy, as we shall see later, is the question of national discipline. If we wish to build up a strong economy, there are no short cuts. For example, economies are built through national savings and a people's aptitude for saving is a matter of discipline. In the face of this kind of problem, democracy as a political method presents tremendous problems in that it is not primarily designed to enforce national discipline. For a developing society therefore, the key to the problem of the democratic method may be expressed in this way: how does one arrive at national consensus in a political methodology that begins with the assumption that the right to dissent has logical priority over the need for consensus?

There are no easy ways around this problem. A developing society that has chosen the democratic road must face this issue squarely. Since a developing society has to harness its will to the accomplishment of urgent tasks and since it cannot afford to fail in those tasks, its leaders must learn to accept the paramount importance of the national good in certain situations. If they are unwilling or unable to do this, they may be certain that the democratic process will fail; indeed will be inevitably self-defeating if those who operate within the parameters of freedom which the system allows are incapable of learning self-discipline in the interest of national purposes. Therefore, the challenge of the democratic method in a developing society is to see whether one can preserve the right of dissent, encourage the recognition of personal responsibility and isolate the areas of collective action that demand national consensus.

Obviously, in the totalitarian system with its emphasis on unity, organized consensus and management might make some aspects of the process of rapid transformation easier of accomplishment. But other prices would have to be paid in terms of individual liberty and further disadvantages might soon surface such as a stifling of the spirit of individual initiative. In any event, speculation about the respective methods may prove idle if a society takes naturally to one method rather than the other. The problem remains: How does one make the natural method work? We must look at the democratic process itself and see whether we can detect in it operational weaknesses which might be corrected.

Let us consider two particular features of democracy and ask the question whether they are necessary for its functioning or merely bad habits that have grown up through the uncritical neglect of those who have operated under the system. First of all, let us consider the idea of the relationship between those who hold power as a consequence of elections, and are subject to periodic recall, and the people they govern. Most democracies have shown an increasing tendency to treat the group that is elected to power as a dictatorship legitimized by the electoral

B

process because of the assumption that everybody will obey the constitution that requires this. This may have had the effect of freeing elected governments to act without much regard to popular participation and understanding; but it has also had the negative effect of leading to an increasing separation of governments and what they seek to achieve on the one hand, and popular understanding and hence, the will to perform, on the other. In this context political parties have been seen as 'vote-getting' machines rather than as instruments of communication between governments and people and people and governments. Obviously, where the social condition demands change, which in turn, requires the mobilization of the understanding and the will of the people, this method of operation is highly undesirable. In fact, it is not surprising that the impatient idealists, who begin with the assumption that this is an organic part of the system, should conclude that it is the system itself which is incapable of change. But is this so? Obviously not. What this method of operation has reflected is a long period in history in which democracy has happened to be concerned with what we earlier described as the politics of tinkering and has not happened to be concerned with the politics of dynamic change. This is not a criticism of the system. It is only a comment upon the uses to which the system has been traditionally put. Later we will consider the role of the political party in a democratic system where the objective is dynamic change. For the moment, I content myself with the comment that it is not the system that is at fault, but the people who have used it. Unless otherwise prodded, men will tend to abdicate the responsibility for vigilance and participation in the democratic process. But the answer is not necessarily to abolish democracy, but rather to adapt is operational methods to the challenges of change.

Let us now consider another and perhaps more fundamental aspect of the problem. If change is to be accomplished, people must be mobilized. But mobilization does not imply 'dragooning'. What it implies is the acceptance by institutional leadership and by people generally of the need to make special efforts to achieve special purposes. Now, one of the seriously irrelevant features of many democratic systems, and of the Jamaican system in particular, has been the tendency to assume that every single identifiable group in the society is in some vague, dimly-comprehended, but almost instinctive way at war with every other group. Workers are naturally at war with employers and vice versa. Industrialists are sure that they are at war with the government, even if they cannot quite put their finger on the battlefield. Teachers will teach but against a half-instinctive, half-articulated background of hostility to the government which pays them. All this, derives from a number of things, all of which, I suggest, begin with misconceptions. For example, there is the assumption that because *laissez-faire* capitalism was founded in the notion of competition and because democratic politics were, for a long period of time, associated with *laissez-faire* capitalism, that this combines to mean that the democratic system works necessarily in a climate of institutional 'brinkmanship' in which the whole society is always on the verge of an explosion. A moment's reflection will indicate that there is a profound non sequitur in this process of reasoning. To begin with, *laissez-faire* capitalism as understood in the middle of the nineteenth century is already an institution that shares its proper place with the dinosaurs in our natural museums. Its skeleton may not yet actually be on display, but it is in fact there, to those with sufficient historical perception. To assume, therefore, that democracy as a method of political organization must suffer from the defects of *laissez-faire* capitalism represents not so much the acceptance of a natural condition as a total failure to adapt one's political perceptions.

Granted this broad historical background to the problem, one must look most particularly at how our difficulties were exacerbated by the colonial experience. Having already inherited, through colonialism, the worst competitive irrelevancies of *laissez-faire* capitalism, our problems were further compounded by the fact that political power was exercized by remote control through a governor. In these circumstances, the question of a sense of unity in national purposes became a contradiction in terms. Obviously, where power was totally centralized in one man and manipulated from four thousand miles away, every institution was necessarily in competition with the government and thus a climate was induced in which all institutions quite logically assumed that they were also in competition with each other. This latter was necessarily so, because the thought that all institutions could come together for a common national purpose did not occur to anyone until well into the twentieth century. Thus, the leaders of institutions regarded themselves as, first, in conflict with the colonial authority for favours; and second, and more disastrously, in competition with each other for those favours.

Hence, already cast in an antagonistic mould by the influence of nineteenth-century capitalism, colonialism lent special force to the habit by investing it with an institutional logic of its own. It is as if the society regards itself as organized into a permanent adversary system. Once again, the question is whether these attitudes are fundamental to the system or whether they are excrescences that have developed by historical accident.

I suggest that they are accidental features of the system. I suggest that since the system itself represents the natural tendency of the society one's duty is to consider how to adapt the system so as to make it relevant to a morally-oriented politics of change. I intend later to consider the relationship between economic ownership and equality as a totally fundamental exercise. I will also examine the question of how the democratic system can be made to operate, retaining idealistic consistency in terms of freedom of dissent, while pursuing an operational method which achieves collective action through constant popular participation. I will contend that it is the 'politics of participation' which will permit the mobilization of people and institutions behind national programmes aimed at proclaimed social objectives that command national consensus. The economic problem we will discuss in terms of the democratization of ownership.

I will contend also, that the goal of equality at the political level is best realized through the democratic system when conceived in terms of a participatory method of operation.

3

Equality

ECONOMIC and political power within the social group, interact upon each other. It is irrelevant to consider which leads to the other. The fact is that the possession of either tends to lead to the acquisition of the other. Control of the ultimate sanction of force facilitates the acquisition of property, and the possession of property makes it possible to gain control over the instruments of force. Thus control of either force or property leads to the concentration of power in the hands of a minority. This, in turn, leads to the formation of classes and soon there is added to raw distinctions of power, the more subtle workings of social and psychological exclusiveness. Manners are refined and the refinement particularized to the power minority. Add to this the desire to pass privilege from parent to child and we soon have the picture of hereditary class distinctions. Here, then, the path to an egalitarian society is blocked not only by the facts of minority power but strewn with the debris of a thousand subtle forms of attitudinal conditioning.

As we consider how to dismantle the apparatus of privilege it is necessary first to define what is meant by *equality*. It may be simpler to begin with the process of exclusion. Obviously, one does not mean that men and women are born with equal talents or aptitudes; that everyone is going to make a contribution to the society of equal complexity; and that everyone is going to need the same degree of training to be able to perform different functions. What is meant, however, is that everyone in a society must begin with a sense of equal worth. In the same way, a society must value equally every human being within its purview.

One of the great problems of social organization is that there is a paradox inherent in this equation. If all do not have equal talents nor make contributions of equal complexity how then can they be of equal value?

This contradiction lies at the heart of much of the confusion that has surrounded political thinking over the ages. It certainly lies at the heart of the distinction between the attitudes that are proclaimed by politicians and the reality of social relationships within a particular social and economic organism. The question of how to resolve this paradox involves one of the most difficult of all the intellectual perceptions which man must master. I often find myself when faced with this paradox, going back to ultimate simplicities in the human experience.

The only way in which I think I can attempt an explanation is to go back to instinctive patterns of parental reaction within a family. A mother and father never measure their love for their children by intelligence quotients or performance. If they do, they are unworthy of the privilege of parenthood. Great parents love all their children equally, and have an equal place in their hearts for every child that is the fruit of their union. And they will watch some children come first in their class and others break records in the field of sport and yet others achieve nothing more than average citizenship; and yet on birthdays and at Christmas, in pain and in sorrow, in triumph and in crisis each child will weigh equally in the heart and the consideration of the parent. Society is, as every African knows, an extension of the family and therefore, for societies to be moral, they have to achieve in their extended context, the same instinctive moral sense of the worth of every member of the family.

This is not, I fear, any high-flown philosphical projection; and yet I suspect it is the only approach to the problem which provides a simple foundation for the notion of an egalitarian society. Therefore, I suggest that a society is egalitarian when every single member feels instinctively, unhesitatingly and unreservedly that his or her essential worth is recognized and that there is a foundation of rights upon which his or her interests can safely rest.

Let us consider some of the practical implications of this. When a child is born, an egalitarian society must first of all ensure equality of opportunity. I shall consider later some of the implications of this idea for economic organizations in areas like housing, welfare and social security. In the present context however, let us examine education, social mobility and class attitudes. I choose these three because they seem to be more fundamental to the enterprise of equality than anything else.

I suggest that no society can approach the organization of

equality except within the framework of a single, integrated educational system. This is so because equality must imply, in the most literal sense, that it is possible for a man to rise as high as his innate talents permit. It also implies his automatic social acceptance at any level of the socio-economic scale which he attains by virtue of his talents.

Therefore, those who seek an egalitarian society must first address their minds to the question of the organization of one stream of education through which all must pass. This means that the children of attorneys, doctors, prime ministers, governors-general and street cleaners must go through one stream of basic primary, secondary and tertiary education. Economic reality and natural selection may place limits upon how far each child can proceed along the road of educational opportunity. Resources may not permit the provision of a secondary education for every child today. Similarly, even fewer may be able to aspire to a university education. But the objective must be crystal clear: all children must pass through similarly endowed institutions wherein they must mix, regardless of parental background, and from which they must proceed to higher levels on the basis of merit alone.

When it is insisted that all children must share this common experience, the first foundation of the egalitarian instinct will have been laid. By this means there will be established as a firm fact in the mind of every citizen in early childhood, which is the time when their attitudes are fashioned, that each must make his own way in life and that superiority in terms of performance and circumstance cannot be inherited but must always be earned.

I go further and suggest that it is accepted that the process of natural selection will see some children climbing higher on the ladder of education in subsequent performance than others. However, each must nonetheless be taught the lesson of equality and shared responsibility in and for the nation. Therefore, we must search for a mechanism through which those who have been most successful in the educational system along with the average and the least successful are joined in a period of working together for the national good. Later I will discuss the importance of this for the notion of social responsibility and its implications for the spirit of self-reliance. For now, it is enough to insist that a single educational system is critical to egalitarianism. It is by this means that we can teach the first lesson which is that parental accomplishment does not confer a privileged status upon children. There remains the danger, however, that superior performance within the educational system may lead a child to an elitist conclusion in its own mind. A period of national service in which the most brilliant university graduate must share the experience of common service with a child who is not likely to rise higher than a shop floor foreman, may refurbish the first lesson and give it a new and salutary relevance before the student passes finally out into the mainstream of adult existence.

This leads us to the question of social mobility. Implicit in the entire argument is the idea of total upward and downward economic mobility. No society is egalitarian unless the street cleaner's son has an equal chance to become the chairman of the the board of the largest corporation in the land. Equally, egalitarianism is not approached unless the son of the chairman of the board of the largest corporation in the land may end up in a factory because that is the position which his talents entitle him to occupy. This is a bitter pill for people to swallow because it cuts across the grain of the parental assumption of transferred benefit. But the truth is that parents only assume that it is their duty to elevate their children beyond the entitlement of skill because society places a different weight and a different value upon the different occupations within it. If society accepted the equal, intrinsic worth of all its economic functions, parents would not fall into the trap of what may be described as 'elitist manoeuvring' on behalf of their children. There is a sense then in which societies and parents have trapped each other in an immoral cycle of cause and effect, all of which work against the possibility of egalitarianism. But if we assume that economic mobility is the proper consequence of the notion of equality, then we must attach to that assumption a consideration of social mobility. By social mobility we mean not only that a man can buy a larger house because of his greater skills, but also that he will be accepted instinctively by others who already have larger houses should he move up the scale. Equally it means that he will continue to accept those with smaller houses that he may have known in his previous situation.

I realize that these are still totally challenging and perhaps seemingly revolutionary notions for a society like Jamaica. However, this does not invalidate the ideas. Rather it is an implied condemnation of the assumptions upon which Jamaica's social attitudes now rest. The fact is that in Jamaica and indeed all over the world there is great resistance to the social acceptance of people whose upward mobility is the result of their economic skills. Equally, there is the almost universal tendency of those who have experienced upward economic mobility to forget their friends and associates on another rung in the economic ladder. But if we are even remotely concerned with the notion of a just society founded in equality we must address our minds to all the strategic and tactical requirements of attaching to economic mobility the reality of social mobility, in the sense of accepting people naturally and easily as people, rather than as symbols of economic accomplishment and traditional status.

This leads to the question of class attitudes. The idea of class is as old as Plato who gave it the ultimate intellectual sanction of a superb mind. His *Republic* reflected his observation of the social realities of his time and was concerned with the question of inspired leadership, elitist continuity and the fact that division of labour implies that there must be somebody to do the dirty work of society. However, the analysis, though dazzling in its crystalline symmetry is irrelevant to the realities of power in today's world which has been conditioned, first by the industrial and cybernetic revolutions and, second by the insertion into man's philosophic equations of the idea of equality as a natural outcropping, in social terms, of monotheism. If there is a Fatherhood of God that is indivisible, then there is a Brotherhood of Man that is not subject to degrees and fractions. Therefore, the persistence of class stratification is unacceptable morally, divisive socially, obstructionist economically and a source of tension which if not removed, will inevitably provoke social instability.

Clearly, the hierarchical structures which reflect economic necessity must never be allowed to harden into social classes. Further, if we can evolve a mobile social system the claims of authority and order can be met without violence to the principle of equality. But to achieve this, we must work consciously towards a kind of society which is like our family model in which there are no classes of children, but only children of different skills enjoying different rewards, but with equal claims upon parental love and concern.

4

Self-Reliance and the
Problem of Attitudes

I TURN now to the question of self-reliance. At the outset, it is very important to establish certain distinctions as they relate to the concept. It would be easy, for example, to fall into the trap of confusing self-reliance with selfishness or social indifference. Needless to say the concept does not imply either of these things. Self-reliance is perhaps best identified as implying the recognition by every human being of his ultimate responsibility for himself in his social context and to himself in the course of his life. As the old saying goes: You can take a horse to water, but you cannot make him drink. Equally, you can devise the finest educational system in the world and it remains the case that each child must make a gift to opportunity of themselves if the process is to succeed. Naturally, home environment, parental influence, good teachers in a basic school system will all contribute to the probability of a child responding to opportunity. Behind all this, however, lies an ultimate and entirely private responsibility which cannot be escaped if men are to respond to life with achievement.

Equally, societies have got to develop a similar sense of shared responsibility. If one takes the case of the individual in his group it can easily be seen that there is no contradiction between self-reliance and a sense of social responsibility. The former refers to our capacity to accept responsibility for our own development within the social grouping; while the latter implies our awareness that our development must take place in the context of a general respect for the interests of others in the group. So, too, with nations.

Self-reliance implies the ability on the part of the people of a country to make common efforts towards the general development and welfare of the group. This has its counterpart in a sense of international responsibility which is the recognition that the interest of each nation must be sought in the context of a larger appreciation of the interests and welfare of mankind as a whole. When one reflects, history is replete with examples of forces that have tended to promote self-reliance; and, equally, it is besmirched with examples of forces that have tended to undermine man's search for independence of spirit.

The classic example of a social equation that destroys the spirit of self-reliance at every level is to be found in slavery. For the slave, the experience presents a simple choice between independence of spirit and instant punishment. The persistent assertion of 'independence' leads inevitably to death, and it is the spirit of self-reliance that shares the coffin. But equally, the institution of slavery undermines the spirit of self-reliance in the slavemaster since it is of the essence of the slave system that the master achieves performance through someone else. The master escapes his own responsibility to perform by compelling others to perform on his behalf. In the end, both are trapped in a cycle of despair; and both are destroyed – the only difference being that the slave is destroyed in spirit and body, while for the master, the destruction of the spirit is masked by the body's escape.

At the international level, colonialism is an extension of the slave-master relationship as between classes within a society to the larger scale of the relationships between entire peoples and nations. I suggest, therefore, that the consequences of the relationship as between nations locked in the colonial equation is markedly similar to those that arise amongst people locked in the slave equation. Here, of course, one has used slavery as an example only. It must be remembered that the master-servant, superior-inferior relationship has taken many forms in history.

European feudalism, czarist despotism, Latin American military dictatorships operating at the behest of an oligarchy, South African apartheid and Dixiecrat racism are all variants of a common theme. Similarly, colonialism in the sense of the rule of one people by another is an extreme form of a generalized historical phenomenon in which societies, for one reason or another, are externally dominated. Thus, one must make distinctions within a common category to understand history. If one thinks that our distinctions imply a difference of category, one may fail to understand history. The common factor between the relationships in a feudal system and those in a slave system must be identified if the effect upon the human spirit which they share in common is to be understood. Equally, one must understand the similarities between a colony in the old political sense of external rule and a society which, nominally free in political and constitutional terms, is nonetheless so subject to external economic and cultural domination as to reduce its apparent independence to impotence. Many countries which have escaped from political colonialism have celebrated the event with an enthusiasm that quickly subsides as it becomes apparent that the newly acquired freedom was more illusory than real. So much for the negative side of the coin.

As Hegel divined philosophically, and as every physicist since Newton knows as a matter of course, history is the story of action and reaction.

The Pharaohs held the Jews in bondage and so there arose, with historical inevitability, a Moses as man's first recorded symbol of the spirit of self-reliance. Thereafter, the Old Testament is devoted to the story of the self-reliance of a people struggling with an hostile environment. It is fascinating to observe that the Jews saw much of their history in terms of divine punishment for any deviation from that path. It is one of the great ironies of history that the spirit of self-reliance propelled the great migratory tides which led to the displacement of the Indians as the owners of the North American continent. The frontiersmen who opened up the American continent for development by the use of what was originally a European technology, were a classic example of self-reliant man. So, too, was the Indian hunter whom the settler replaced because of his access to a more advanced military technology. These men are to be contrasted with another type of human being who has been conditioned to demand and expect nothing of himself. This type of man assumes that he has a 'lot' in life, expects to rest securely on somebody else's efforts and looks to 'the powers that be' to ameliorate his condition. As we have observed before, men who have been conditioned by the colonial experience tend to the second type because, colonialism, by definition, separates men from access to power and so destroys their acceptance of responsibility.

Societies achieve in direct proportion to the total output of all their members. This applies to communities within societies, and to nations in the context of the international community. The great challenge in a society like Jamaica is how to develop this sense of personal responsibility, for one's own development subject only to the proviso: I am my brother's keeper. The lack of this spirit is the most difficult of the legacies of our past to undo. But, our success here will determine whether anything else is possible. This is not only important if we are to release the society's individual and collective capacity for performance. It is also the only path along which the individual may walk to true personal satisfaction, since man is only truly happy when he discovers his own creativity.

In considering the whole question of self-reliance, it is important to examine specific problems of attitude in the society. Take attitudes to work, for example. In Jamaica, the sons of the privileged are never in any circumstances seen doing certain kinds of work. No matter how 'good for nothing' they may be, the system operates to maintain them in a position above the need for menial or dirty work. The sons of the poor observe this happening, generation after generation, and know also that often they have to tackle these jobs even if their abilities entitle them to a higher position in life. By a process of historical association, therefore, certain kinds of work, in addition to being unpleasant, become associated with poverty and relegation to a section of the social scale. Thus, wherever the ability to avoid certain kinds of work becomes a traditional right handed down through the generations and exclusive to an identifiable class or group within a society, it is inevitable that a stigma will attach to those kinds of work in the view of the rest of the society. When added to this is the further dimension of a long experience of slavery as part of the historical background, there are the makings of a serious attitudinal problem in relation to work.

Unquestionably, the effect of slavery upon Jamaican attitudes must not be underestimated and should never be ignored. There are many who would prefer to console themselves by suggesting that it is bad to dwell in the past. Certainly I would concede that one must not take up permanent residence in the past. However, if one seeks to understand the social dynamics of today, one must trace the major processes of history. Anyone who has ever opened his ears to the language of the Jamaican people is struck by the persistent tendency to describe as 'slave driving' an injunction, or even an appeal, to work harder provided the call comes from those in authority. We at once realize that the recollection of slavery passing from generation to generation still looms large in the consciousness of those who regard themselves as working class. In addition, for nearly a century and a half the working class have observed that the sons of the so-called middle and upper classes have never, in any circumstances whatsoever, had to perform the tough, manual tasks of society. Small wonder that there is a partly unconscious, but always simmering resentment of those forces in the society that seem to condemn other men's sons permanently to those tasks.

This resentment often leads the unthinking upper and middle classes to dismiss the rest of the population as 'lazy'. Doubtless, those who use the term successfully conceal from themselves the historical injustice that is implied in their own privilege, and they comfort themselves with the assumption of a hereditary superiority. However, both the conclusion and the assumptions upon which it rests are inaccurate and stupid. The fact of the matter is that the Jamaican small farmer whose forbears escaped from the sugar estates to the hills after slavery, is one of the hardest working men in the world. He springs from the same stock as those who are described as 'lazy'. Equally, those who are described as lazy have a working record that is unsurpassed whenever they are outside the Jamaican milieu. Ask any Florida farmer his view of West Indian farm labour and he will rhapsodize. Ask any native New Yorker or Britisher about the capacity of the Jamaican working-class migrant for work and his response will reflect a mixture of astonished admiration and resentment of the fact that the migrant upsets time-honoured standards of reasonable maximum work outputs per day. Also one has to distinguish between a Jamaican working for others and one working on his own account.

Anyone who has watched an 'own account' tailor in Kingston and observed the hours of unbroken concentration of which he is capable, will realize that this is a man of exceptional stamina, energy and application. Clearly then, work attitudes insofar as they are negative in a society like Jamaica, reflect internal social tensions that do not respond to censorious injunctions, hectoring, bullying, nor exhortation. It is more prudent to begin with an analytical comprehension of the social forces that have produced this state of tension.

Obviously, the long-term reconstruction of society in terms of that upward social and downward economic mobility that are fundamental to egalitarianism will provide the only enduring answer to the problem of work attitudes. Equally, the educational process must be designed to incorporate an early indoctrination of all children to accept the inherent worth of all types of work. Unfortunately, however, our problem cannot await the long-term solutions that are inherent in the reconstruction of society. Once again, one must resort to shock tactics that are designed to compel a reconsideration of attitudes and their modification in response to the power of example. This is why it is vital for political leadership to 'back its jacket' and get in among the people at the roughest working levels from time to time. However much it shocks the establishment, prime ministers and other political leaders must set the example of setting aside times when they mix cement and push wheelbarrows and handle a shovel. Apart from being good for the physical condition of the leaders concerned, this makes an important symbolic point which repeated often enough will begin to inspire a new view of work generally. Nor is this any idle theoretical gesture. The fact of the matter is that a mayor who will get up at 5.00 in the morning, ride a street cleaning truck and shovel muck with his men inspires them to an entirely new view of their own worth and the value of what they do. It is a brutal society that would condemn a man both to dirty work and to the feeling that the work itself belittles the man. Yet this is the sort of social distortion to which we are condemned by the acquired attitudes and values of class-stratified elitist social forms. Therefore the assault must be both symbolic and practical and should spread throughout the entire functioning of the economy. It is not only politicians who should set this example. Industrial managers should do the same. Any fledgling personnel officer can tell you that a factory manager who will get out on the shop floor from time to time and, particularly in times of crisis when there are major breakdowns in equipment, gets a response in terms of both goodwill and productivity which far outweigh any practical contribution that he can make to the particular job in hand. Equally, those who manage from within the leather-padded, air-conditioned fortress of their office, remain permanently at a loss to understand the ill temper and sagging productivity of the worker who batters in the heat and endures the clatter and din of the shop floor. Hence, if we wish both goodwill and productivity, the egalitarian method in which the rough and the smooth are to some extent shared is not only morally compelling but effective.

There is a sense in which the symbolic act of working together is a necessary prelude to an effective challenge to the spirit of self-reliance. Where we have, for example, brought into a single national focus the business of sharing labour on a particular national holiday, we find that we release within people an instinct for self-help in community action which sets the stage for the more systematic development of self-reliance. Once again, of course, the long-term answer to self-reliance lies in the educational process. But even in the short run one can stimulate a national mood that leads to practical beginnings.

Here the key lies, once again, in the appeal to the communal instinct which lurks in the wings of the average man's consciousness, waiting to be summoned to action. This is particularly true of a country like Jamaica which displays to a remarkable degree an instinct for 'good works'. If a Jamaican worker is suspended without pay, it is natural for his brothers on the job to rally with voluntary contributions and make up his pay. Urban communities in Jamaica have survived in spite of crippling rates of unemployment through one of the great, voluntary, social welfare systems of the world known as 'share-pot' or 'partner'. In 'share-pot' the families of a tenement yard literally keep each other alive by sharing their meals as between those who are employed and those who are unemployed at any given moment. Even the service clubs, like Rotary, Kiwanis, Lions and the rest have demonstrated a remarkable capacity for the voluntary financing of basic schools, children's crêches and the like. Before any attempt at mobilizing a national attitude, Jamaicans have displayed at all levels of the society this aptitude for voluntary co-operation. The fact that this may have been seen unconsciously in terms of charity, and may have reflected as much a concern for social stability as a passion for justice, is neither here nor there. The fact is that the instinct is present and can be released into a completely different kind of national involvement if it can be led to operate within a clear social focus.

It is important here, however, to distinguish between two things. On the one hand, there is the desire of those who have benefited from the society to give something back as their own contribution, rather than merely to depend on governments to correct all social evils. This represents one form of self-reliance springing from one motivational pattern. Separately, there is the question of self-reliance on the part of those who have not really benefited from society. Here again, one finds an instinct of community co-operation which can be harnessed in a national way. The old tradition of work days on which neighbouring farmers would gather to help one of their number is eloquent testimony to this spirit. This profound social impulse for survival through self-help and co-operation which we described as 'share-pot' is another case in point. So on all sides the psychological raw material is present.

The political challenge is how to draw it all together so that it provides the foundation for total national efforts. This leads one immediately to the question of identifying priorities so that one may seek to focus the will of a society on a particular identifiable project. A classic example of such a project can be found in a national assault upon the problem of illiteracy. By the start of the decade of the 1970s, exactly one quarter of the total Jamaican population were functionally illiterate. This is in itself an affront to the very idea of social justice. Equally, it represents an abdication of any possibility of major social and economic development since you cannot help to develop a society in a situation where one quarter of its members have been denied the most critical single tool of modern civilization. The identification of illiteracy as a major impediment to progress is a relatively simple matter. What is more challenging is to summon up the will to overcome the problem in a predetermined period of time. But if you are to hope to succeed, it is a challenge that must be met. One might be tempted to feel that both the challenge and its solution have a merely technical implication in the sense of providing an entire population with the basic tools with which to develop both themselves and their environment. If one reflects, however, one is soon struck by the fact that there is a deeper challenge and a deeper opportunity.

In the immediate post-colonial period, a country may not have any single event in its history to which it can point with unqualified pride. Apart from the attainment of independence itself, it is in the nature of colonialism that it affords few opportunities for self-congratulation. Yet a sense of one's capacity to achieve is fundamental to the development of a national spirit. Therefore, here, as in other cases, one must shock a society by the nature of the challenge that you present to it. Thus, quite apart from the technical implications of an early achievement of total literacy, one is also concerned with a number of equally important imponderables. The bringing together of a whole society to work for a single, visible, national objective like total literacy represents a first call to arms, a rallying point with which people can identify and to which they can commit the best of themselves individually and collectively. Even more importantly, the accomplishment of the goal will represent for the nation a great point of pride in achievement which will begin the long process by which you overcome the problem of a national sense of inferiority. It is my own judgement that this last, this pride in accomplishment is the most important of all the consequences that will flow from a successful outcome to a national battle of this sort.

It is not for nothing that every Englishman finds within himself a level of response to the exploits of Marlborough, the Battle of Waterloo and the defeat of the Luftwaffe in the Battle of Britain. The truth is that all people need an heroic image of themselves if they are to be capable of heroic response. In societies like Jamaica, the heroic episodes of our past are far too few. Therefore, government today must not only reflect the politics which have been described as the art of the possible. It must reflect also the pursuit of the 'impossible', so that our own capacity may be confirmed to ourselves and self-doubt banished.

5

Social Justice

I HAVE suggested that self-reliance, equality and democracy are the objectives towards which we must strive. Without these we cannot build a 'just society'. Let us now consider what is meant by the term 'just society'. Any political system which claims a moral purpose must be concerned with social justice. This is defined as a form of social organization consciously seeking to regulate the relations between all its members in a manner that is predictable, capable of rational exposition and taking into account the equal weight of each member's claim upon the total organism. I have used the term 'predictable' because social justice cannot exist where decisions are arbitrary. I have referred to 'rational exposition' because, obviously, social organization is dynamic and its relationships are subject to change. If there is to be justice, however, 'change' must be capable of rational exposition acceptable to the people at large. Finally, I refer to the equality of individual claims as a reminder of the assertion that is fundamental to my thesis: the egalitarianism is the only enduring moral basis for social orgnization.

Granted the assumptions implied in predictability, rationality and equality, how can one envisage a model of society towards which one can constantly strive in the hope that the steps of the journey will be predictable because they are rational, and rational because they lead to equality? I suggest that one must begin by recognizing that the basic unit of human existence is the individual. Despite all the modern social philosophies that have sought to dazzle us with concepts of the state and of society and which suggest that a number of people acting in concert take on a super characteristic that is larger than the sum total of the individuals themselves, I remain an unrepentant disbeliever. For me, social organization was created by individuals and exists to serve the needs of those individuals. The fact that individual need is often best served by the imposition of collective discipline

51

is a pragmatic phenomenon involving no mysteries and implying no mystical collectivities with their own separate personalities.

This distinction, which is at the heart of the age-old debate
about democracy and totalitarianism, is completely fundamental
to any consideration of social justice. Granted that individuals in
a social group must always surrender a degree of individual right
to collective need, the question turns on whether the degree and
extent of the surrender are the result of conscious acts
subject to modification from time to time through some process of collective decision-making. If this is so, then the state
of the relationships within the society reflects that society's
capacity to organize just relationships at a given moment in time.
If, on the other hand, relations in the society are ordered by
any other means, they represent the imposition upon the whole
of an arbitrary judgment which does not reflect a collective
consensus. The fact that a society in the latter circumstances may
appear to be more just in a number of respects than a comparable
society of the first kind, does not alter the fundamental proposition. History is replete with examples of benevolent despotism
doing good works. The problem arises precisely at the point
where benevolence departs and despotism remains. Who defends
the people then?

It is my contention that the people are best able to defend
themselves in the long run of history. Therefore, a society is best
able to organize justice for itself when it is consciously organized
on the basis that everyone should have access to the decision-
making process. It is only when the decision-making process is
accessible that one can assume that decision-making will be
steadfastly dedicated to the organization of justice, as between
individuals and as between each individual and society as a
whole.

Let us consider the question: What are the basic elements of
a just society? This can only be analyzed in terms of individual
human experience and need. Perhaps it can be most simply
expressed by asserting that a society is just to the extent that it
makes available to all its members, those things that are necessary
to human happiness. Essentially, human happiness can be said to
rest on four sets of foundations: one is material or concrete; the
second is psychological; the third might be said to be both concrete and psychological; and the fourth is the means by which

the members of a society can be made capable of achieving the first three.

In the area of the material or concrete one can isolate three main elements. First, a society must be so organized as to provide for every willing and able citizen an opportunity for work. The ability to earn a livelihood through the sweat of one's brow is the most fundamental of all the pre-conditions of human happiness. Where this opportunity does not exist, all the other human rights will tend to take on the quality of fantasy. In view of the vast complexity of individual human aptitude as against the needs of society, the organization of economic opportunity for everyone is, and will continue to be, the most challenging technical problem facing modern man. But success in this field is fundamental to the search for social justice and it must always stand at the very centre of political and social concern.

There is, then, the question of the three essentials of civilized existence: food, shelter and clothing. The place that these three occupy in political concern represents a paradox. There is no modern politician who does not pay lip service to the primacy of the claim for food, shelter and clothing. Yet in nation after nation, the record of performance in this regard is abysmal. The United States and Russia will commit vast resources to the exploration of outer space while both tolerate extensive ghettos with inadequate housing. Jamaica permits upper-crust housing developments of entirely unrealistic splendour while the shanty towns of Kingston and Montego Bay mock the very notion of social justice.

In the case of nutrition, large areas of the world are in the grip of feeding problems that range from severe protein shortage to outright malnutrition. This is happening while North American grain surpluses languish in their silos and, equally, while Jamaica has allowed idle hands and idle acres to co-exist for a decade of her new-found independence.

Finally, in the area of material need is that group of remedial protections which are often described as 'cradle to grave' security. There are a number of problems that attach to the human condition which are predictable and which represent man's continuing vulnerability in his environment. Throughout life it is possible to predict a series of problems that beset mankind. Mothers need calcium and phosphates and vitamins in the pre-

natal period. Babies need special care if they are to survive.
Young children need to be inoculated. At all ages teeth require
care. Working men become too ill to work for periods and
need both medical and economic help during their difficulties.
Technological processes change so that people with one set of
skills become redundant and must be supported while they are
trained for reabsorption into the economic process. Some people
are either born handicapped or suffer permanent disability later
on. They must be cared for, and trained to play a part, however
small.

In the end, old age comes to most of us and it behoves a
society to make this time of final transition both comfortable and
dignified. It is a necessary extension of egalitarianism that a
society set aside the means to provide for all these problems of
the human condition. All this calls for a formidable degree of
planning. It also calls for substantial sacrifices on the part of
the able-bodied, together with the foresight to recognize that
individual tragedy, like old age, is no respecter of persons. It can
truly be said that the instinct for equality is reflected in the
social conscience of a nation. The kinds of welfare provisions
which deal with human vulnerability are the anatomy of social
conscience.

Let us now turn to the second set of foundations: the psychological aspects of social justice. Here, of course, categories are
harder to define, but if one considers the nature of human
experience it becomes possible to detect levels of need which
must be met if the individual is to have a chance of a full and
happy life. Here, I distinguish three major areas of concern.
First, the individual must have an opportunity to be involved in
the decision-making processes of the society. Obviously, every
individual is involved in a personal decision-making process
throughout his life. In addition, most individuals take part in
decision-making processes at the family level. Often the needs of
the individual and those of the family appear to be in conflict and
give rise to considerable personal strain and tension. However,
experience indicates that where the members of a family feel
involved in the larger decision-making process, much of the
tension disappears, because a dialogue develops between the
individual and the group processes. The kind of happy relationship that exists in families that maintain this dialogue springs

from the satisfaction of both a practical and a psychological need.

At the practical level a family may decide to walk an extra mile of sacrifice because it discovers that a promising son deserves a chance to take a post-graduate course. Or, again, the group may chip in to finance a holiday which might save their daughter's marriage. These may seem to be trivial examples but they go to the heart of the idea of individual and group dialogue to the practical advantage of all. Behind the practical looms the more fundamental question of the psychological satisfaction that derives from the feeling that you can influence your environment. In our first example, the son who gets his post-graduate course lives ever after in the certainty that his group respected and valued his talent. His group lives thereafter in the knowledge that they liberated one of their members to a fuller exploration of his talents. All feel a personal inter-connection and sense of creative responsibility for each other.

The principles that are illustrated by this simple analogy of the family are no less true when one considers the larger grouping of society. At both the political and the economic level it is critical to the creation of a just society that the individual should feel involved in the decision-making process. Naturally, in the large and complex relationships of modern societies organized on the basis of the nation state, it is extremely difficult to devise institutions and working methods which ensure this involvement. However, in my view, it is a task from which one must not shrink. Both at the practical and psychological level individuals and families must feel capable of influencing the political and economic decisions which provide the social frame within which the same individuals and families must take their personal and group decisions. Thus, a primary aim of social organization must be to secure that the relationships between individual and family and family and society all share the common characteristics of dialogue leading to influence in the taking of decisions.

After the question of decision-making in this category of psychological importance, I wish to consider the 'sense of belonging'. If we go back to our model of the family and consider any normal, well-adjusted family group, one can observe a characteristic that is shared by all. Every member of that family is able to take for granted their equal worth in comparison with any other member. In sickness each member can assume that the rest will rally. In education, each child can take for granted that the group will go as far as resources permit to ensure that the best training is made available. If resources cannot stretch to meet the needs of all the children, it can be assumed that the choices and the exclusions have some rational basis. Thus, both in action and in the psychological assumptions which may be made, all members of the group feel themselves to be of equal worth in an instinctively egalitarian organism. This is the quality of feeling and experience which must exist among all the members of a society if it is to lay any claim to the reality of social justice.

This is to throw down the gauntlet finally and irrevocably to all theories of social organization that involve elitist assumptions. Here, one means by the term 'elitist' a system in which people are entitled to advantages as a consequence of being born to a privileged and supposedly superior group; or, alternatively, that people become subject to different laws as a reward for exceptional merit. In this context an egalitarian society implies that excellence may be measured in the reward but does not alter the equality of each man's status before the law; and equally that ability and performance should be the sole criterion for the receipt of special reward. It is my contention that elitism and social justice are mutually exclusive. Equally, I assert that no elitist model of society is capable of achieving true social justice. I so contend because the mere fact of elitism contradicts the notion of equality and *ipso facto* makes the organization of social justice impossible. Further, I suggest that even a well-intentioned elite justifying its existence as a transitional phenomenon and declaring its ultimate intention to be egalitarian, will be defeated in the end by the fact of its own superior status, by the workings upon its own character of the power that it possesses, and by its inability to escape from the prison of its own advantage. I believe that Acton enunciated a permanent truth of human nature with his famous remark about the corruption of power.[1] Therefore, the commitment to the view that every member of society must have equal weight and value, must be total and unswerving.

[1]'Power tends to corrupt, and absolute power corrupts absolutely. Great men are almost always bad men.' Lord Acton (John Emerich Dalberg 1834-1902) in a letter to Bishop Mandell Creighton (1887).

Of course, when one looks at any society in the world today, one is driven almost to despair. So great is the gap between the egalitarian ideal and the actual experience. There is the tragedy of the black minority in the United States. The Communist Party in Russia is one of the most tightly organized and privileged elites in the world. In Jamaica the so-called middle class represents a highly entrenched enclave of privilege, and urban masses are substantially disadvantaged and do not, in fact, feel that they are individually or collectively of equal weight in the society. To this must be added the further complication of race. While superficially accepting the notion of a multi-racial society, the truth is that Jamaica is not yet at peace with blackness or comfortable with its African heritage. A cold evaluation of relationships within the Jamaican society reveals a series of imbalances. The fact is that people with light complexions enjoy a psychological advantage and consciously or unconsciously have assumed an additional 'weight' in the society. In the case of people of dark complexions, the reverse has been the case. To an even greater extent people born to middle class families enjoy both practical and psychological advantages of a substantial nature. Those born to the poor suffer the reverse. All this demands a consideration of strategies which may quietly dismantle the apparatus of privilege and replace it with a dynamic social organization designed to provide the channels of opportunity for talent regardless of origin, an atmosphere of equal worth, regardless of talent, and a sense of ease with and pride in all the streams of our ethnic origin.

Third in this category, we must consider the question of the creative use of leisure. Of all the aspects of a just society, this is the most elusive. It is my conviction, however, that human happiness is attained through the development of three levels of experience. One is to do with the building of families as the group frame within which the seed of Adam is passed from generation to generation. Then there is the business of providing which involves pride and satisfaction in work and involvement in the decision-making processes which determine the nature of, and rewards for, work. But also, there is the question of leisure and personal fulfilment through the use of leisure. Here, we must be concerned not so much with the provision of leisure which is already guaranteed as an automatic by-product of modern economic organization. Rather I am thinking of the development of intellectual tastes and the self-confidence to use leisure time to develop those sensibilities of the mind which are not necessarily engaged by the economic process. The development of the individual who can not only enjoy being entertained by a football or boxing match but who can also explore the human condition, and his own, through reading, looking at sculpture and painting, listening to music, or coming to grips with a play or a dance recital, is vital to a fully developed experience of life. It is also important to social justice itself since it is probable that wider intellectual development leads to a greater consciousness of the very issues that are at stake in the building of a just society.

I now turn to the third category which I described as partly psychological and partly material: the position of the law in a society. Much has been written about the rule of law. Obviously, the non-arbitrary and rational foundations of a just society are enshrined in the system of laws, the methods by which they are adapted and the procedures under which they are administered. The relevant concepts here are too massively documented to bear repetition by me. The independence of the judiciary, the legislative process and the concept of equality before the law are categories which we take for granted as fundamental to the rule of law. But sometimes we take them for granted at our peril. In the case of Jamaica, for example, we may be able to assume the independence, integrity and impartiality of the judiciary. We can certainly take for granted the propriety of our legislative processes. But can we really say that each man has equal access to the remedies of the law? A most superficial observation of the system at work refutes any such claim. Very often unconscious class prejudice seems to lead to summary justice of the worst kind when some poor boy is hauled before the courts. Inherent in the adversary system is the fact that wealth has a better chance of victory than poverty. The free legal aid service which is supposed to correct the imbalances of the adversary system covers a limited range of cases and tends to make available to the poor client only those who may be regarded as comparative failures among the practitioners of the profession, together with the inexperienced. As a consequence, the poor do not have equality before the law; and, what is worse, they know it. Thus, once again, we have both a practical and a psychological invasion of that 'sense of equal worth' which is such an important element in a just society.

There is also to be taken into account, the state of the laws themselves. As a consequence of the fact that our colonial rule coincided with the great period of *laissez-faire* capitalism in metropolitan history, our laws still reflect a savage bias in favour of property as distinct from people. It is incredible to observe that in the year 1972 the punishment for the theft of property could be greater than for the kidnapping of a child. Equally, an examination of laws as they affect landlords and tenants or in relation to hire purchase agreements and the repossession of property all indicate this bias. Perhaps this is nowhere more dramatically illustrated than in a bankruptcy case. In such cases, all creditors in relation to property such as goods not paid for and the like, have a preferred status under the law and have a right to the realizable assets of the firm in liquidation. But workers with that firm who may have given their entire lives to its service have no claim whatsoever, not even for wages owed, vacation leave unpaid, not even for contractual obligations for severance pay, arising out of formal union negotiations.

In a just society, property exists to serve men and not men to serve property. Obviously, the individual must have a right to own property and this right must be reflected in the law. But this ownership must stand in a reasonable relationship to the rights of the people at large, because it is the sum total of all those individuals that make up the whole society. The rights of each must be reflected equally in the objectives which the law must seek to serve, the method by which it operates and the manifest impartiality with which it affects everyone.

We turn, finally, to the fourth category: the means by which these objectives must be secured. This, obviously, is through the process of education. The educational system in the context of the search for a just society is dealt with in Part II, Chapter 4. To accomplish this quest, substantial modification is required in both the objectives and the methods of education. But suffice it to say that the search will be fruitless if it does not begin with a critical evaluation of what education is designed to achieve and if there is not the determination to tackle the business of equality, in every sense of the term, from this early vantage point.

One, then, might summarize social justice as being concerned with the organization of access. There must be equal access to jobs, to food, clothing and shelter; to social security; to the decision-making process; to the sense of belonging and being of equal value; to creative leisure; to the processes and remedies of the law, and to education. Men are not equally gifted but they are severally endowed and to each there must be accorded access to society's opportunities.

PART II

The Strategy of Change

Introduction

I HAVE sought to define a moral frame, a social objective and a possible methodology for our political system. The rest of the book will be devoted in the main to the consideration of strategies aimed at accomplishing the changes that are necessary for the transformation of the society.

I will not attempt any quantitative analysis of what is required. I will not be dealing with growth rates or gross national product, the rate of school construction and the like. This book attempts a qualitative assessment of our situation and seeks to suggest strategies as they relate to the adaptation of the quality and style of life that are a necessary part of a just society. Quantification is the business of the technician. Quality of life is the business of the philosopher. It is the politician's task to bring to bear upon the philosopher's objectives the technical expertise that can support a life of quality upon an adequate material base in terms of the production and distribution of goods and services. However, the politician would be unable to order his priorities and would be confused by the technical options which are presented to him, if he had not made his peace with a social philosophy that is at once moral in its structure and relevant in its appreciation of the possible.

I have suggested that any attempt at the politics of change will fail if it is not supported by popular will. But popular will can only be mobilized in a context of understanding. In the post-colonial world, understanding can be difficult to come by in popular terms, because of the accumulated confusions that are induced by the colonial experience. People's attitudes are profoundly influenced by colonialism which often produces a value system that is totally at variance with the kinds of attitudes that are necessary to construct a just society. Equally, one must distinguish another problem. It is not only that colonialism produces false values. At an even more profound level, it can be said that any situation which has separated people from power and responsibility for a long period of time undermines individual and collective self-confidence. Any kind of despotism will do this, and to the extent that colonialism is an externally manipulated despotism, it has precisely the same result. Thus when we look at the attitudinal climate within which we must attempt change, we find on the one hand, that we are confronted by a false value system and on the other, a condition that verges upon national inferiority complex.

Thus in a strategy of change, the initial assault has got to be upon the value system and the first attempts at psychological reconstruction must be aimed at the problem of inferiority complex. It might be as well here to consider a few examples of both those problems so that we can better illustrate some of the practical requirements in any strategic assault upon them.

First, there is the example of what is sometimes described as the appetite for conspicuous consumption. This attitude includes the assumption that there is a right of access to consumer goods regardless of productive contribution. It expresses itself in an unthinking appetite for and preoccupation with consumer goods, but a disinterest in productive responsibility.

Second, we must remember the problem posed by the individual and the collective assumption that responsibility for the solution of problems lies in other hands. Third, we can observe attitudes to work which are characterized by the assumption that a general stigma attaches to certain kinds of work, particularly those that depend upon the use of the hands or involve working the land; indeed anything that does not conform to either the professional aspirations, or that pattern of escape from reality that is symbolized by a preoccupation with the white collar job. One can, once more, make a number of reasonably valid assumptions about the historical processes that produce these attitudes, but must face the fact that they are inconsistent with the possibiliy of building a society upon viable economic foundations. Here it must also be observed that since it takes a wide spectrum of jobs to make an economy function, an egalitarian society cannot be built if our value system condemns a number of its functionaries to an automatic contempt because society itself will not accept the inherent dignity of every job.

Finally, we must consider the more generalized problem of the inferiority complex. One must look a little more closely at the historical process to understand the impact of colonialism upon attitudes. At an obvious level, the very fact that one people can conquer another seems to provide a type of superficial proof of a superiority-inferiority relationship which inevitably will leave scars upon the psyche of the conquered. To this we must add the psychologically debilitating effect of the superior technology which the Western metropolitan powers brought to bear in the process of colonial economic exploitation. Then there is the fact of the dislocation of the cultural continuum which colonialism visits upon the subject people, and the displacement of local cultural systems by those of the conquerors. Here one must constantly remind oneself that it is not enough to be privately secure in the knowledge that local art and culture have as enduring a validity as the metropolitan form. On the contrary, there is, for the majority of a subject people, the danger that the implied superiority of conquest itself invests the conqueror and all his works with the quality of superiority. Hence the tendency of formerly dependent people to reflect two opposite but similar tendencies. There is the tendency to copy everything from the accent, and the literature, to the manners of the conqueror. Alternatively, there is the more positive, certainly more declamatory and possibly equally invalid tendency to repudiate all the ways of the conqueror and to invest the ways of the conquered with a quality of exclusive truth that owes more to the need for defiance than of objective truth.

Thus, the politics of change are likely to find themselves stuck in a quagmire if one does not begin with a clear-eyed appreciation of the problem in terms of its historical origins, present confusion and future possibilities. In the course of this, one must distinguish the arenas in which the battle must be fought. Some of the battles are negative in the sense that the conflict is aimed at the deliberate break-up of those attitudes which by being rooted in the colonial trauma represent clear impediments to the release of an indigenous creative spirit. Other battles have to be fought in the positive arena of releasing attitudes which are in themselves creative and upon which one can rest the thrust for change and development.

If one looks at the negative side first, one cannot escape the necessity to throw down the gauntlet to the past. For example, let us take the question of dress. There are those who would delude themselves into feeling that concern with styles of dress is a childish waste of time. Not so. It is by no means the beginning or the end of the problem, but it has its place. If you live, for example, in a tropical country, that has acquired the jacket and tie as a style of dress for that country, you have made a number of unconscious concessions. First of all, you have adopted as your own a style of dress that is not suited to your climate. This is the first act of psychological surrender, since common sense would dictate that a style of dress should reflect the reality of the physical environment. Further, the very fact that you did not question the relevance of another man's style of dress to your physical environment is a confession of a paralysis of judgement. Third, where the style of dress is inherently expensive, you have placed a strain upon the ability of your society to create the external symbols of egalitarianism. Fourth, where the style of dress has become associated with the status symbol of class and the escape from economic reality through the 'white collar' syndrome, you have inhibited your own ability to identify reality and placed yet another psychological obstacle in the path of a realistic pursuit of your own social and economic possibilities.

In the face of this, your first duty is to challenge the chain that ties tomorrow's possibilities to yesterday's conclusions. The task is to break the chain even at the price of shocking the society. Indeed, it is desirable that one should shock the society, because only by the act of shocking are you likely to generate a form of collective introspection through which people will begin to re-examine the basic workings of their own unconscious assumptions.

The strategy of change must, accordingly, operate at the psychological and attitudinal level which involves a concept of mass education; at the structural level which involves a concept of social and economic organization; at a political level which involves a concept of mobilization; and it must envisage the problems of transition which involves a capacity for tactical accommodation. It is in this context that I will, in succeeding chapters, attempt to examine some of the problems that arise in the political system, the structure of the economy, the relevance of our foreign relations, the quality of our education and the nature of our institutions.

The Politics of Participation

JUST as a one-party state can mobilize by abolishing dissent, equally, I suggest, multi-party democracy can mobilize by abolishing remoteness. If we regard the right to dissent as too priceless to be curtailed, then we must discover our solutions within the other half of our dilemma. To do this we must begin by asking ourselves two questions. First, does government have to be remote? Second, can we make it intimate?

Obviously, the sheer size and complexity of modern government presents us with a problem of increasing difficulty. To begin with the size of government alone creates an ever-growing bureaucracy which increasingly separates the politician from the people. Then again the world changes so rapidly that governments often find themselves confronted by problems which no election manifesto could anticipate. All this tends to drive the politician into an increasing isolation from which he governs in a mood of mounting authoritarianism, hoping that somehow he will justify it all at the next election.

When we set this trend in the context of our earlier analysis of competitively oriented societies, we can readily see how difficult of accomplishment is any spirit of national co-operation. However, neither the one-party state nor the acceptance of the *status quo* are adequate solutions for a society like Jamaica's.

An alternative method must be sought and it is, I suggest, best described as the 'politics of participation'. The antithesis of remoteness is involvement. Since remoteness is the problem that we must tackle, involvement must be the objective of our method – by involvement I mean the conscious attempt to make people feel that they have a part to play in the decision-making processes of government. At this moment in history most democracies create a sense of popular involvement at election time, but the involvement tends to focus on, at best, two aspects of the total governmental process. These are the determination of an election manifesto and the election of a party to form a government. Thereafter, it is understood that the manifesto will become increasingly irrelevant while the government becomes increasingly remote. What is needed, however, is to create the institutions through which people feel continuously involved in the decision-making processes as these unfold in response to the interplay between idealistic commitment and realistic challenge.

This sense of involvement is critical, because no matter how deep the idealistic commitment of a government, it faces real and often unforeseen difficulties that sometimes force it into compromise or unpopular decisions, or into calls for sacrifice that may not have been anticipated at the time of an election. Very often, the choice is between a compromise of objectives and a call for sacrifice. Where there is no popular involvement in the decision-making process a government will tend to compromise. Where there is popular involvement, a government may find itself emboldened to call for sacrifice. And it is here that we come to the heart of the problem of the politics of change. To have the strength not to compromise derives partly from the sheer political will of the leadership that is involved; but more importantly it derives from the capacity to mobilize people to an understanding and acceptance of the necessity for special effort and sacrifice.

Obviously, we do not mean by the 'politics of participation' that we must hold a referendum every time we face a crisis of decision. What we do mean, however, is that we must genuinely seek to involve the country in the decision-making process. I would like to look at four specific areas in which one can consciously create both the fact and the appearance of involvement in the decision-making processes of government. Later we will show how the sense of popular involvement must extend into every aspect of social and economic organization, but for the moment, we are considering the problem of government isolation.

The four areas that must be examined are, how the government relates to the people at large; how it relates to institutional leadership; how it decentralizes its own operations; and finally, how it relates to the political organization which put it in power and must, hopefully, maintain it there.

The question of how a government relates to the people at large, is, perhaps, the most difficult to discuss. Since we cannot govern by referendum, all that we can discuss here is a style of communication. One may, however, distinguish certain imperatives. First of all the members of a government must proceed with manifest integrity and humility. Obviously, if integrity is suspect, the call for sacrifice will evoke mockery; and where there is arrogance, the merest attempt at communication will arouse resentment. Then there is the matter of honesty. There has to be total commitment to frankness and a willingness to take unending pains to explain problems, objectives and methods. Perhaps in societies that can take for granted the integrity of institutional and national leadership, this emphasis will seem strange. However, many societies with a long historical experience of slavery have been marked by the experience in subtle ways. The slave-master relationship does not permit of any moral formulation because it is in itself unnatural and immoral. To a lesser extent, the same is true of the relationships in colonialism. Where a relationship is inherently immoral, it is inevitable that the circumvention of the relationship by fair means or foul, should become the only relevant motive for human action. This has led to the symbol of Anancy, the spider of folklore who survived by outwitting all those set in authority above him.

The discovery of moral foundations for social action is, in this context, a long and painful business, the outcome of which can never be assumed just as the objective must be constantly pursued. This is a vastly time-consuming business but is part of a price that one must gladly pay for maintaining confidence and understanding. Equally, one must be willing to listen and consciously create devices by which the views of people can be heard and their suggestions actively sought, carefully analyzed and courteously acknowledged. All of these things taken together can do much to maintain a climate of confidence by building an atmosphere of dialogue between government and people.

I shall now turn to the relationship between government and institutions. It is vital to create mechanisms and operational methods through which institutional leadership is genuinely involved in the decision-making process. This can be accomplished at two levels. In the first place, one must actively organize throughout government leadership a constant dialogue with the leaders of institutions such as manufacturers, farmers, traders and trade unionists. These bodies should always be consulted when major problems loom and their advice not only sought, but listened to and when possible acted upon. For example, if a government wants to launch an unpopular programme, such as restricting imports, it can proceed in one of two ways. Acting from its position of authority, it can announce which products are banned, give an explanation and leave it at that. This course will have inevitable consequences. There will be resentment of what appears to be autocratic, however legitimate. In addition, the government will soon find itself submerged with protests as merchants who are affected begin laying off sales and other staff, partly because they are genuinely affected by the ban, but partly to reflect a general mood of pique. In the end, the purpose of the ban will become lost in a babble of frictional confusion. An alternative method is to call in all the firms who might be affected, explain the difficulties that have led to the decision and ask them to help you analyze and sort out the problems that will be created by the ban. In this way, one can anticipate problems and even, perhaps arrange the smooth transfer of affected staff to other fields in the general mood of co-operation and joint planning that will prevail.

At a more precise level one must build into all the planning mechanisms of government an element of institutional participation. For example, an economic planning council must be supported by advisory committees in which the politician, the government technician and the relevant institutional leadership meet regularly to discuss and plan. This gives to a government the opportunity to explain to sectoral leaders problems that arise from a total view of the nation's situation as well as the part which a particular sector is expected to play in the drive for overall national objectives. Equally, the leaders of a sector have an opportunity to explain their particular difficulties and to feel that their worth as contributors to the total national effort is recognized. An important by-product of the entire process is that it challenges sectoral leadership to focus its attention upon creative initiatives as well as immediate problems. This, then, is the method of involvement which must extend to education and teachers, health services and doctors and so on throughout the system.

However, the tendency of all modern government is towards centralization. It is an axiom of government that de-centralization is the key to a sense of popular involvement. This is what makes the institution of local government so important to the democratic process. Of course, there have been those who have argued that a country like Jamaica is too small to support both a local and a central government structure. This line of reasoning suffers from two defects. First of all, it assumes that a centralized system will necessarily lead to the optimum use of resources. Second, it assumes that small nations provide only one level at which the individual identifies with a group. Taking these assumptions in turn, we may safely dismiss the first, since all evidence shows that de-centralization of authority and function is critical to the maintenance of efficiency as central governments grow in response to the ever-increasing complexity of the challenges with which they must deal. Turning to the second assumption: it is safe to say within reason that wherever people identify themselves with a section of a country in a manner that may be distinguished from their identification with the country as a whole, there is a basis for local government.

The only question that can still arise is whether the sub-group with which they identify is large enough to support some kind of governmental structure. In the case of Jamaica, for example, where there are fourteen parishes, it is unquestionably the case that people see themselves in terms of a parish identification as well as a national one. It so happens that a Jamaican parish is a large enough entity to support a government structure. Therefore, the conditions for a local government structure at both the practical and psychological levels exist. Provided these conditions exist, it is clearly good for the democratic process to have a local government structure because it is within this structure that you find the most immediate and practical answer to the problem of remoteness in government. By its very nature, local government deals with the sorts of problems that arise from the 'felt needs' of a people. Street cleaning, street lights, pot-holes, water supplies – these are the basic human priorities which people need most and often feel most strongly about. These are the sorts of things that local government is ideally suited to provide. More importantly, the geographical unit within which these things must be provided is small enough to permit a sense of intimacy between people and government at that level.

In Jamaica we have to completely restructure our local government. To be effective, this kind of government, like any other, must have both the responsibility and the power to respond to the people's needs. By a curious historical oversight, however, the Jamaican local government system is unique in the world. One has often heard of governments that have had power without responsibility. Our local government system is, I think, the only one in the world in which there is responsibility without power. In the Jamaican system we go through the charade of electing a local government authority. The law defines a number of areas in which this authority is responsible. It provides that the local authority can do absolutely nothing without the express permission of a department of central government. For example, the citizens of a village may be concerned about the state of the road which serves their needs. It applies to the local government authority for repairs to be made. The local government authority may agree that the case is urgent and will prepare plans to deal with the problem. Those plans, however, have got to be submitted to a ministry of local government for approval before the actual work on the road can commence. If the central government approves the expenditure, all is well. Since the power resides ultimately at the centre, however, it is possible that the central government may turn down the proposal. If this happens and it often does, the villagers who want their road fixed confront a local government authority which they blame for non-performance in the first instance. The local authority responds by explaining that the real blame attaches to the central government. In the end the villagers probably find it difficult to decide who to believe and may resolve the dilemma by dismissing both local and central government along with whichever political party happens to control either or both, as a set of liars and rogues.

Clearly, this is bad for the democratic process which should always provide a clear means of identifying responsibility so that praise and blame may attach rationally and with good cause. Needless to say, a bewildered electorate is never quite able to decide who is to blame for failures of performance; and not uncommonly, ends by saying 'a plague on both your houses', meaning by 'houses' both the local and the central authority. All this adds up to a prescription for popular cynicism.

The reason behind this confusion is in itself a fascinating commentary on colonialism. In the days when all authority was exercised by a colonial governor, government was merely the instrument through which his will was translated into action. Where there was no power attaching to a central government answerable to the people, it followed that there could be no power for a local government answerable to the people. However, upon attaining independence we provided ourselves with a central government answerable to the people, but completely forgot that a similar exercise was due for our local government bodies. These were, by oversight, attached to the newly-created and independent institution of central government in the same state of paralyzed subservience which they had endured in their relations with the colonial governors of the past. However, the solution is both simple and necessary for the development of the politics of participation. Defined autonomy for local government is necessary for its effective functioning and important for the development of the politics of participation.

Here it is appropriate to consider the question of regional planning. If the process of involvement is to be pressed into new areas of opportunity one must seek to stimulate means by which people generate ideas for development on their own. In this regard we are dealing with both the dynamics of participation and the stimulation of self-reliance. It is not enough for the politics of change that skilfully devised plans for integrated economic and social development should be centrally hatched for subsequent implementation in a particular area. The people of an area must be encouraged to think for themselves and come up with ideas for their own development which can be subsequently refined and rendered feasible by centrally located technicians. Nor is it beyond the wit of man to devise an operational method which creates this sense of dialogue between the people of a region and the central planning process. It is vital that the institutions to make this process possible should be devised because the key to mobilization is involvement and the key to involvement is the sense of joint authorship.

Let us turn to the question of the political party. Left to themselves, political parties quickly degenerate into machines for attacking opponents, distributing the spoils of office and electing candidates. Political reality demands that one deals with one's opponents. But he who becomes preoccupied with his opponents quickly surrenders to a bankruptcy of moral purpose. The politics of change calls for the ability to walk up a tough and winding road. Anyone who has ever walked up a tough and winding road looking back over his shoulder to swap insults with the bystanders that he passes will soon miss a turn and fall over the precipice.

Consider the question of the distribution of favours. The attitude that is implied by the term, 'to the victor, the spoils', is understandable. Once again, however, the politics of change demand a different focus. If the purpose of politics is the distribution of favours, one had better make sure that there are enough favours to go round or those who are not favoured will rise up in due course and smite those who are. But if one's vision is limited to the distribution of spoils one will have neither the imagination nor the energy to build an economy with enough to go round. Thus, the politics of change demand that energies be saved for the creation of wealth at the economic level and the equitable distribution of that wealth at the social level. Any other policy is folly.

Naturally, political parties exist, in part, to elect candidates to office. But they lose the capacity for action in power to the extent that they become dominated by this primary consideration. Indeed, many of the problems of a political party in a country like Jamaica arise from the very forces of history that have tended to create the dependency syndrome. Very quickly political parties become another manifestation of that syndrome. Left to itself the party will soon be seen as a short cut to externally provided solutions. Once this particular rot sets in, the political party ceases to be an agent of change and becomes merely another instrument for the preservation of our post-colonial paralysis. The only answer is to be found in perceiving two additional and over-riding functions for a political party. One is to recognize it primarily as an instrument of mass political education. The other is to develop its potential as a two-way instrument of communication between the people and the government.

In terms of its educational function, a political party must have a clearly articulated philosophy, a precisely defined set of social objectives and a broadly conceived political strategy. A large share of its activities should be devoted to the dissemination of these ideas along with their constant discussion so that adaptations of strategy can reflect the accumulated wisdom and common sense of the people themselves. And here we must be quite clear about what is and what is not subject to adaptation. The philosophy of an egalitarian society is a non-negotiable item. You are either an elitist, an egalitarian or unconscious. A party of change cannot by definition be unconscious. It must therefore choose between the elitist and the egalitarian model. Once committed, there is no more room for change.

Social objectives flow from philosophy and are equally resistant to adaptation. Therefore, it is only in the area of political strategy that there is room for the revision of technique. And it is here precisely that one must be as sensitive and as flexible as one is rigid and inexorable in the pursuit of basic principles. It is in this context that we must view the role of the political party as the means through which dialogue is maintained between government and people. This represents an interesting but not insurmountable challenge to the Westminster model of democracy. Here, as in so much else in life, the problem is one of communication. The notion of a rigid separation between a cabinet of government and the executive of a political party has no necessarily permanent foundation. All government institutions represent a pragmatic response to reality. The problem arises where today's responses were born out of yesterday's realities and ignore today's problems. What is needed is to devise a series of formalized occasions and institutions through which cabinet government and its various ministers are in constant dialogue with their equivalents in the structure of the political party. This, in turn, requires that the dialogue flow upward and downward through the total political machine. In the last analysis, what is required is a new perception of the purpose of political organization together with the wit and the will to make that purpose work.

The 'politics of participation', therefore, involves the attempt to make government the beneficiary of institutional advice and responsive to popular need. Its tools are communication and dialogue, its method involvement, and its purpose mobilization.

2

The Restructuring of a
Post-Colonial Economy

ONE cannot, in the course of a chapter, attempt a major analysis of Jamaican economic problems either in isolation or in relation to the general Third World condition. Instead, I will try to identify some of the major problems which we have inherited, and to indicate some fundamental objectives along with strategic priorities, if these objectives are to be accomplished. Again, my purpose is to deal with categories and concepts rather than specific issues.

Discussion of an economy and its development is only meaningful if it takes place in the context of defined objectives. Before attempting an analysis of Jamaican economic problems and strategies, I should like to suggest therefore a set of economic objectives as being fundamental to the building of a just society. The five basic considerations in the analysis of an economy are:

    i   The growth of the economy
   ii   the distribution of wealth
  iii   the ownership of resources
   iv   the control of resources
    v   the utilization of resources.

I will consider them in the context of the view that, where the commitment is to social justice, economic activity must serve the needs and interests of the whole social group. In addition, these factors are all subject to the first objective of a just society which is to ensure that every family has the capacity to feed, clothe and house itself which in turn implies that each family has access to remunerative employment which is capable of providing these things. Food, clothing and shelter are the cornerstones upon which the economics of social justice must rest.

When one talks of the 'growth' of an economy, one refers to the rate at which it increases its output of goods and services. Human ambition being what it is, it is obviously important to maintain a substantial rate of growth since increases in an individual's standard of living tend to whet the appetite for more. Where, in addition to the phenomenon of escalating consumer appetite, one can add genuine problems of poverty and a rising population, the rate of economic growth becomes critical.

However, the growth of an economy can be meaningless in terms of a just society if the distribution of wealth is not equitable. A common feature of societies embarking upon the post-colonial adventure has been gross maldistribution of wealth. Obviously, then, equitable distribution of wealth is a precondition of social justice in any country and takes on a peculiar urgency in most post-colonial societies and certainly in Jamaica.

It is impossible to modify the distribution of wealth without considering the ownership of resources. Where the means of production are concentrated in a few hands, it is inevitable that wealth will tend to accumulate in those hands at the expense of the rest of the population. In addition, both the rate and the character of economic growth will be affected by the ingenuity, energy and sense of public responsibility of the few who own, bearing in mind that these qualities decline in direct proportion to the length of undisturbed possession. Thus, all oligarchies tend to become less productive and socially relevant as time passes.

Any analysis of the ownership of resources must bear in mind the distinction between ownership and control. Resources may be widely or narrowly owned. They may be concentrated predominantly in a few local or foreign hands. Ownership may have a predominantly family, co-operative or corporate character. However, whatever the pattern of ownership may be, there remains a separate and vital question of how resources are controlled. A minor illustration of this important distinction can be provided by a comparison of the influence upon a company's policy of shareholders on the one hand, and a managing director and his team of technocrats, on the other. Shareholders may own, but technocrats control. At a far more fundamental level however, we must consider the question of whether economic policy is consistent with defined and articulated national goals. Since economic policy and performance are substantially influenced by the separate behaviour of the various productive, trading and other units of the total economy, the question of broad, public control is critical if these policies are to form part of a coherently orchestrated national effort.

The purpose of controlling the use of resources is to ensure their optimum utilization. Where resources are efficiently and imaginatively used growth rates will be maximized. Hence, economic efficiency is a function of resource utilization. Equally, social justice is itself affected by this question. At its most fundamental level, resource utilization is the foundation of social justice. The most important resource in any society is its people. Those same people represent the purpose behind the organization of social justice. Therefore, if a part of the people are unemployed we are both under-utilizing the nation's basic resource and denying the possibility of social justice.

To summarize, then, the Jamaican economy must grow and distribute its proceeds equitably. To do this its system of ownership must be consistent with national objectives and its resources must be controlled to ensure that they are used to the full and in a manner consistent with social justice.

1945-1972 – AN ASSESSMENT

To understand many of today's economic dilemmas one must begin with a broad assessment of Jamaica's economic situation as it existed in 1945. After some three hundred years of British rule and more than one hundred years out of slavery, Jamaican society displayed eight basic characteristics. Most of these features are to be found in other post-colonial societies and each represents a challenge to be overcome, or at least mitigated, if a just and efficient society is to be achieved.

Export-Import Orientation Perhaps the most characteristic of all the common features of colonial economies is the tendency towards export-import orientation. By this we mean that the total of exports and imports occupy a disproportionately large share of the total economy. By comparison, goods and services produced locally for local consumption make up a comparatively

small share of the economy. The reasons for this are well understood. Colonial territories were developed to supply raw materials,
or, at best, partially processed goods and to act as a market for
the sophisticated manufactured exports of the metropolitan
powers.

A good example of the extent to which colonial Jamaica was
developed in response to its trading patterns with the United
Kingdom is to be found in the administrative structure under
which the island was governed. The island was divided into fourteen parishes, many of which had a port which existed for the
sole purpose of exporting local agricultural products to the United
Kingdom and as the point at which British manufactured goods
were received. Historians have remarked that the parish capitals
which were based on these ports, often had more in common
with London than with Kingston, so great was the metropolitan
orientation of the economy, the political system and, indeed, the
entire society.

Local production for local use was actively discouraged since
production of this sort could only take place at the expense of
metropolitan exports. In Jamaica's case our exports, even as late
as 1945 were exclusively agricultural, consisting of semi-
processed sugar, bananas, together with lesser crops such as
citrus, coffee, cocoa and pimento. It was a minor but typical
irony of our situation that we shipped crude sugar and coffee
beans to England where both were processed and re-exported to
Jamaica. This pattern had two inevitable consequences. First, it
meant that Jamaica like all other post-colonial countries was at
the mercy of the adverse movement in the terms of trade between primary producing and manufacturing countries. Historically the prices for primary products such as sugar, bananas and
the like tend to be unstable but show no general tendency to rise
through time. On the contrary, the prices for manufactured goods
tend to be stable within the context of a general upward trend. In
consequence, as the generations passed, it took more and more
sugar to buy a tractor, a turbine or a motor car. However, the
limits imposed by geography on economic acreages that cannot
be used to produce sugar, bananas and the like make it impossible to produce more and more sugar. Thus, economies like
Jamaica's are trapped in a vicious circle unless they find the
means to break out of the pattern which they have inherited.

The second consequence that is inherent in this situation is that of growing unemployment. Granted reasonably full utilization of economic acreages for export agriculture, one can assume at best a constant labour force. It is more likely, however, that there will be a dwindling labour force as producers turn to sophisticated technology in their battle with rising costs and stagnant prices. In this regard the vicious circle can be illustrated with this example. A sugar producer has to import his fertilizers and tractors. As time passes both cost him more. But the country to which he sells the sugar does not pay him more, so he imports a new piece of labour-saving equipment to try to hold the line on costs. This displaces labour. In due course he has to replace the labour-saving machine, but discovers that he cannot finance the purchase out of his depreciation fund, because the price has soared. So he borrows money to purchase not only the replacement but a further piece of labour-saving equipment. This displaces even more labour. And so the disastrous spiral continues. Where the rest of the economy reflects no dynamic growth, unemployment will rise, not only as consequence of population growth, but reflecting absolute displacement of labour, as well.

The Trader Mentality The natural concomitant of the export-import orientation pattern is the trader mentality. Custom and habit are polite terms for the unconscious brainwashing of the historical process. For three centuries, the economic horizons of the Jamaican were bounded by the production of basic crops for export, on the one hand, and the importation of the total range of consumer goods, on the other. To this could be added an interest in the professions such as law, medicine and the Civil Service. The peasant farmer struggling to make a living by coaxing marginal hillside land to produce root crops complete the picture.

The trader mentality has had a number of consequences. Partly it is a consequence of colonialism; and partly it has itself contributed to the psychological and economic deformities which are associated with the colonial experience. In fact, when one considers the general effect of colonialism and the specific effect of the trader mentality, one sees an example of a major historical force creating a minor phenomenon which in turn helps to perpetuate the efforts of the major force. It is like a variant of the hen and egg theme.

Of course, the most obvious consequence of the trader mentality is that it limits economic activity to the business of distributing imported goods. This places a severe limit on the capacity of the economy to provide jobs and means, in effect, that we are importing other peoples' productive labour. Also, as is the case with export agriculture, the employment potential in the distribution of imported goods tends to be static since one salesman can take an order for two dozen shirts just as effectively as he can for one dozen. Equally, it may take a very large increase in demand before a merchant needs additional delivery trucks, employing extra drivers and sidemen.

Lack of Confidence Colonialism and the trader mentality have had a number of other, perhaps less obvious, but just as debilitating consequences which we must examine. We have already seen, and indeed much has been written about, the extent to which colonialism undermined the confidence of subject people. This was no less true in the economic field. The trader mentality may have begun as the logical response to a single avenue of opportunity. In the end, however, it become a conditioned reflex. By 1945 it occurred to very few Jamaicans that they were capable of producing for themselves. The entire entrepreneurial class was, with a few notable exceptions, in the grip of a paralysis of attitude. As a group, businessmen lacked the will, the inclination and, I suspect, the confidence to tackle simple productive tasks which would satisfy their own needs and engage our resources. This crisis of confidence went even further. It was reflected in the assumption that we were incapable of working out our own solutions to our problems. As a consequence, we tended to revere the foreign expert, not in any rational recognition of his particular expertise, but rather in the manner of a tribesman expecting the witch doctor to produce a miracle. Bound up with this exaggerated faith in metropolitan performance was an assumption that even if we did produce something locally, it would necessarily be of inferior quality. This latter characteristic persists even to the present where foreign goods represent for consumers a sort of status symbol irrespective of rational comparisons of actual price and quality.

A taste for conspicuous consumption is one of the subtler consequences of colonialism, the trader mentality and the general disconnection from responsibility. It is not easy to analyse the precise roots of the frame of mind which this term seeks to describe. It manifests itself in a tendency to spend without regard to one's capacity to pay; more particularly to buy more rather than less expensive goods with an equal disregard for consequences and, finally, in an almost total disregard of the importance of savings.

This pattern reflects, in the first place, a general state of mind. Self-restraint is learned as much through continuing exposure to responsibility as through experience of the consequences of irresponsibility. If an entire people are disconnected from responsibility, it is unlikely that they will show a marked capacity for self-restraint. To this general psychological background must be added the effect of exposure to the consumer patterns of metropolitan countries with their far more advanced economies and higher standards of living. Part of the indoctrination of colonialism led to the assumption of superior metropolitan values. The consumer patterns of an advanced economy would appear, therefore, to represent a higher order of experience to be emulated at all costs. When one adds the force of supposedly superior example to a general disconnection from the experience of responsibility, it is not too difficult to imagine how the pattern of conspicuous consumption took hold in a country like Jamaica, nor that it should rest upon so fragile an economic base. Obviously, the most disastrous practical consequence of conspicuous consumption is to be found in its effect upon savings. The propensity to save is low, and so the ability to finance our own productive efforts suffers.

The Absence of Linkages This brings us to yet another element in the vicious circle. In an export-import oriented economy that is marked by the trader mentality, coupled with a lack of entrepreneurial confidence and a low propensity to save, it is inevitable that our economy should reflect a striking absence of linkages. By linkages I mean industries that exist for the simple reason that another industry exists. For example, the full utilization of by-product possibilities represent linkages. Since Jamaica grows sugar cane we should not only make raw sugar but should also make refined sugar, confectionery, molasses, rum, citric acid, bagasse board and the like. These are all by-products. Equally, industries that exist to provide the means of packaging or transporting a produce represent linkages. Hence, bags for raw sugar, containers for refined sugar, bottles for rum and so on all represent further economic activity that attaches to those products that flow directly from sugar cane itself. In 1945 the Jamaican economy had virtually no linked industries. This was partly because the linked industries were the preserve of the metropolitan power; and partly because in the atmosphere of colonialism it was not easy to come by the will and the resources to tackle these jobs for oneself. Hence, our sugar cane, to take one example, led to almost as many employment opportunities abroad as it created at home.

Poverty and Value Added It is an economic truism that the further one proceeds along the productive process, the greater is the 'value added' and, hence, the greater the wealth accruing to the supplier of the process. If one traces, for example, the 'value added' at the various stages of the sugar process one finds that it is lowest at the point of reaping the cane and milling to the stage of raw sugar. It is highest at the level of refined sugar, confectionery and the final blending of rum. The same is true as we trace the development of aluminium ingot through its bauxite mining and alumina stages. Obviously then since colonial economies were condemned to the first, or at best the first two stages of production it was inevitable that they were equally condemned to the poorest section of the economic process. When one adds this factor to the factors of export-import orientation and the failure to develop linkages and bear particularly in mind the problems of the terms of trade, one can perceive the basic anatomy of the problem of rich and poor nations. One can also see how important foreign policy is to the economic development of a young nation.

Foreign Capital and Foreign Technology Jamaica is a small island which does not possess great unexplored frontiers in terms of undeveloped land and untapped mineral resources. We have copper but not in deposits which are capable of economic exploitation at this moment in the history of copper technology and marketing. The same is true of iron and there is not, as yet, any sign of oil. Therefore Jamaica must assess the claims of political sovereignty and national independence against the background of economic reality. Without these natural physical advantages and with heavy unemployment, Jamaican economic strategy leaves little room for expansive romanticism. For us, survival and progress are matters of margins. We need foreign capital and we need foreign technology. These must be harnessed to our needs with the greatest skill and ingenuity.

Our great problem is to find the proper balance and mix between foreign capital already in Jamaica, the new capital that we need and the institutions of control and systems of ownership which can ensure that economic development is consistent with national objectives.

In the light of the basic economic problems that we have been discussing, it is hardly surprising that Jamaicans in 1945 should have looked almost exclusively to foreign capital and technology to supply the answers to poverty and unemployment. With savings and self-confidence both minimal, unemployment rampant and poverty viewed from the perspective of a growing awareness of metropolitan standards of living, it seemed that something had to be done and quickly. Foreign capital and the foreign expert loomed as the two critical elements of a *deus ex machina* that seemed perfectly suited to the problem. Nor did it seem at the time that there was any inherent contradiction between the quest for political independence and the increasing foreign economic domination that would result from this strategy. Indeed, it may well be that the excitement of the political quest served to obscure the inner economic reality. This strategy must, however, be at least partly judged in context. Already in 1945 much of the Jamaican economy was in foreign ownership with the United Fruit Company of America and Tate and Lyle of Britain, only two major examples of a substantial metropolitan economic presence. Two obvious consequences of this state of affairs were the subtantial proportion of profits that were exported and the number of economic decisions taken in foreign board rooms which were neither sensitive to nor particularly concerned with Jamaica's problems and needs. An increasing dependence on uncontrolled foreign capital, therefore, could only serve to exacerbate both problems.

Irrelevant Education An important characteristic which we may mention arises in the general field of education. The total educational performance was such as to ensure that the population lacked the basic skills with which to effect the transformation of the economy. The sons of planters and merchants either idled through school safe in the knowledge that they would have the right to do as bad a job as their fathers on the plantation or in the company's store; or if they were of a more serious turn of mind, prepared for careers in one of the professions. The rest of the population fell into one of two categories. Either they received an education that prepared them for the simple arithmetic that would fit them for a sales counter; or, even worse, emerged from the process barely able to read and write. If we total the skills of an indifferent planter, a lazy merchant, a sales clerk and a semi-literate manual worker, it is unlikely that we will find the kind of expertise that can modernize an economy. This explains a paradox of Jamaican history. Great skill in the fields of medicine, the law, politics and even the arts has been demonstrated at the same time as a comparatively weak performance in the area of sophisticated economic growth.

The Gap between Rich and Poor The final characteristic which we must note is a consequence of the distribution of wealth. As a consequence of its economic structure and educational system Jamaica consisted of three almost self-contained societies in 1945. There were the merchants and planters, the first of which had substantial assets and income and the latter substantial assets and uncertain income. Then there were the professionals who had income but no assets; and finally there were the workers and peasants the first of whom had a little income with no assets and the second, little assets with virtually no income. The gap between the first two groups and the last represented an affront to social conscience.

The period from 1945 to 1972 witnessed the attainment of representative government followed by full internal self-government in 1959 and full independence in 1962. During this period the basic model for economic thinkers and planners was to be found in the Puerto Rican experience. Strenuous efforts, including various kinds of incentives were made to attract foreign capital, both in the areas of import substitution and manufactured exports. Later these inducements were spread to include local capital. The bauxite industry was developed on the basis of total foreign ownership redressed by special taxes and comparatively high wages. Special diplomatic efforts were directed towards price supports for our export crops and various devices were employed to funnel financial support to farmers of various sizes. The institutions of a modern economy such as a central bank, industrial and agricultural development corporations and agricultural marketing corporations and the like were created. However, this remarkable flurry of effort did not substantially affect the main problems of 1945 which were massive unemployment and the serious maldistribution of wealth. In fact, both unemployment and the gap between the rich and poor increased during the period.

It might be worthwhile to pause here and consider the eight characteristics which have just been discussed as they were affected by the effort between 1945 and 1972.

Twenty-seven years can seem like a long time to those who live through them and particularly to those who are understandably impatient for change. However, in the broad sweep of history it is a very short time indeed. One's view of the degree of transformation to be observed in the period will be substantially affected by whether one judges purely in terms of concern for change or from the posture of a detached observation of the historical process.

In the matter of the export-import orientation one can observe a considerable growth in the range of internal economic activity. At the same time I was constrained to observe in a speech in 1969 that between the years of 1958 and 1968 the percentage of the gross domestic product represented by imports had actually increased from 32.7 per cent to 42.9 per cent, while exports rose from 21.9 per cent to 25.1 per cent. During this period considerable progress was made in the manufacturing sector. The annual value of locally produced manufactured goods rose from $55.8 million in 1959 to $115.3 million in 1968. Nonetheless the basic problem remained as is shown by the first set of figures.

Similarly, the struggle to free ourselves of the trader mentality has met with mixed success. The burgeoning manufacturing sector is eloquent testimony to a certain degree of success. However, as of 1972 the mercantile community had still largely failed to come to grips with contemporary opportunity. For example, there were by that date few firms which had begun to experiment with backward integration, the process by which a trader begins to produce for himself the things that he sells. A striking example of our continuing susceptibility to the trader mentality is to be found in the relations between cloth merchants and the local textile factory. A textile factory designed primarily for basic cotton fabrics was established at the start of the 1950s. In the ensuing twenty years it had an indifferent record of performance requiring constant doses of protection by government regulation to survive. In all this period that section of the mercantile community that traditionally retailed cloth, complained bitterly and incessantly about the mill. They could always give a masterly analysis of the various shortcomings that could be observed in the mill's operations. Yet throughout the period it never occurred to any of them to propose a take-over of the mill and its reorganization. Indeed when asked this question by me in the form of a challenge in 1972, one half of a representative gathering of cloth merchants thought that my suggestion that they take over the mill and run it to their suit was a joke in dubious taste. The rest looked merely uncomprehending and gave no sign of being amused.

Insofar as confidence is concerned the picture is equally mixed. A young generation of businessmen and executives has emerged in the economy which displays great energy and entrepreneurial skill. However, the sections of the economy which remain under traditional management have been singularly unenterprising and timid. This is particularly true of that huge area of the economy which is still devoted to our traditional export crops. Equally, as I remarked earlier, sales opportunities for local production are still inhibited by a lingering consumer inferiority complex which assumes the superiority of the most shoddy foreign goods.

The field of linkages is one of the weakest aspects of economic development over the period. Perhaps more than anything else this explains the fact of our continuing over-dependence on the export-import pattern. The truth is that development in the manufacturing sector has been considerable but haphazard. No systematic and planned exploration of linkage possibilities has taken place with the result that opportunities go a-begging until someone happens to stumble across them. This is partially, I suspect, the result of a failure to understand the processes of economic development adequately which, in turn, has led to chronic failures of planning.

Obviously, where linkage possibilities are unexplored the problem of having too much of the economy concentrated at the lower ends of the 'value added' scale is bound to continue. Naturally there has been progress in this area as can be shown by the development of our own sugar refinery during the period and the increasing development of alumina production, particularly in the decade of the sixties. By and large, however, we have fallen short of our opportunities in this regard. In fact, as recently as 1970 we witnessed the spectacle of selling our coffee unprocessed to Japan thereby risking the destruction of the famous Blue Mountain brand name. This was entirely due to lack of energy and initiative to embark upon a hard-hitting sales programme to promote our Blue Mountain coffee attractively packaged as a special item which people would feel privileged to purchase. The difference between these two approaches, allied to the fact that we took one rather than the other, tells a considerable story about the success and failure of our recent efforts.

It is in the area of dependence on foreign capital and technology, however, that our performance has been weakest. A period that should have witnessed a steady increase in local control of our economy has, in fact, witnessed the exact reverse. In fact, it is estimated that the net investment income outflow increased from approximately $14.8 million in 1959 to $100.6 million in 1972. Against this must be weighed the Jamaicanisation programme which was launched in the second half of the 1960s. This programme was designed to persuade foreign enterprises such as banks and insurance companies to incorporate their operations locally and make 51 per cent of their shares available on the local stock market. Jamaicanisation has met with a limited success and is fair enough as far as it goes. It has three main weaknesses, however, which need to be understood. First, the local companies are still largely subject to the decision-making processes of the parent company operating out of its metropolitan home base. Second, the acquisition of equity under this programme leads to substantial pressures on our balance of payments and foreign reserves; and finally, the Jamaicanisation programme has done nothing to modify the oligarchic pattern of ownership of local resources. The tendency has been for the same wealthy minority to buy into the newly offered equity and no effective programme has been devised for spreading the base of equity holding further to a conscious programme of democratisation of the ownership of resources.

In the field of education our failure to adapt to the challenges of economic transformation has been so marked and the subject of such profound importance to the entire politics of change that it is discussed in Part II, Chapter 4.

And so we come finally to the gap between rich and poor. During the 1960s it emerged from a series of polemics on the subject, together with a number of more serious analyses of the problem, that in spite of our best efforts the gap between rich and poor was increasing *pari passu* with the apparent growth of the economy as a whole. Along with the fact of mounting unemployment, the most striking consequence of the twenty-seven years between 1945 and 1972 is to be found in this fact. The type of economic strategies that have been adopted have increasingly entrenched what is now identified as the 'two tier' economy. More and more a group of favourably placed industries have created an entrepreneurial and worker aristocracy supported by rapidly increasing salaries and wages. The rest of the economy, which in the main means the agricultural sector along with the unemployed, has remained stationary and often has proved incapable of increasing salaries and wages at a rate even commensurate with rises in the cost of living.

This period has witnessed, therefore, those who participate in the bauxite, tourist and similarly placed industries entering upon a new and unprecedented era of prosperity. The new consumer demand which they have wielded has sparked inflation, disproportionate increases in the import bill and opened up a whole new area of marginal activity based on land speculation and high-cost housing developments. None of this is intended as a criticism of those who have benefited from their new found prosperity and taken logical if short-sighted advantage of its opportunities. While this has been happening, however, agriculture and the other traditional sectors of the economy have been unable to match inflation with the proceeds of their own production. Simultaneously the new, 'show piece' industries have

all been capital intensive, with the exception of the hotel industry, and hence unable to absorb either the increases in the
labour force or even the displaced labour which is the growing
feature of the traditional sector. The end result has been a
widening of the gap between rich and poor coupled with a faster
rate of growth, in terms of numbers, evidenced by the 'poor'
section in comparison with the 'rich'. The social tensions that
result from this process are intolerable and represent a threat to
the existing social order if remedies cannot be found and the
process reversed.

There is no single, simple solution to the problem of economic
transformation. Each country must review its own economic
situation, assess its own problems and its own peculiar attributes.
It must sense the inherent strengths and weaknesses of its own
human attitudes and weigh all this in the context of its international situation and internal political dynamics. However, if
one sees social justice in an egalitarian frame and bears in mind
our five economic concerns, – growth, control, utilization, ownership and distribution of resources – one can hope to isolate the
essential elements of a relevant economic strategy.

At the most superficial, one might almost say sentimental level,
unemployment is a reproach to human conscience. The existence
of the problem demands some level of attention from those who
prepare budgets of expenditure, and, at the very least, the provision of funds for special public works designed to provide employment. However, in the context of a genuine commitment to
social justice, unemployment is more than a reproach. Rather,
its presence suggests a total failure of the economic process to
meet social needs. Hence, any strategy of economic development
must begin with a total commitment to the search for full employment. It implies that all economic planning must begin with
a concern for the engagement of human resources. It implies,
further, that the entire collective ingenuity of the society must
be geared to the creation of employment opportunities through
every available avenue. Where equality is the aim of social
organization, employment must be the central concern of
economic planning. As we shall shortly see, this commitment
involves more than rhetoric and actually has practical implications for the planning process and the employment of technology.

Obviously, major problems of unemployment cannot be permanently cured by works programmes. Permanent answers must be found in the fact and nature of economic growth and through the careful husbanding, cultivation and development of usable resources. It must always be remembered that economic development springs from no miracles. Rather, like genius, it flows from an infinite capacity for taking pains.[1]

DIRECTIONS FOR THE FUTURE

What then, are the things about which one must take pains? One needs to distinguish a number of clear areas each of which calls for a particular type of focus. They are the psychological element, the intellectual element, the questions of how to make planning relevant as an instrument of national needs and whether there are aspects of the economy which by their importance require special thought and attention. In Jamaica's case, at this point in time these would be agriculture, tourism and bauxite. We must then consider development in the context of international relations and foreign policy, together with the issue of foreign capital. Ownership, co-operatives, rural development, growth and incomes distribution all have to be looked at as well. Finally I would like to suggest an economic profile for the future.

THE PSYCHOLOGICAL ELEMENT

I have deliberately chosen to consider the question of the psychological elements first because of the conviction that all human achievement flows from states of mind without which the more

[1] There is now a fairly large literature on the Jamican economy. An excellent survey of the postwar period is contained in O. Jefferson, *The Postwar Economic Development of Jamaica,* Institute of Social and Economic Research, 1972. A more general diagnosis of the development problem is contained in W. Demas, *The Political Economy of the English-speaking Caribbean: A Summary View,* Bridgetown, Caribbean Ecumenical Consultation for Development, 1971.

References for the topics dealt with in this chapter can be found in the reading list shown as Appendix IV in the publication of the Commonwealth Caribbean Regional Secretariat entitled *From Carifta to Caribbean Community.* For example, on the question of foreign investment, one may wish to consult the works listed in the names of Norman Givan, Frank Rampersad, Alister McIntyre & Beverley Watson.

technical elements in human performance cannot develop. For Jamaica the two critical elements are to be found in the areas of confidence and of attitude. Because colonialism undermined confidence, the great need now is to develop a mood of national confidence in which the people at large assume that they have both the duty and the capacity for great achievement. This involves the feeling on the part of the investor that he will help create the conditions of success for his own investment by the very fact of investing successfully in his own country. On the one hand, this implies a belief that one can affect one's environment by one's own action. And on the other, it implies the belief that one has the skill to make a success of the particular task to which one applies oneself. There is a subtle interdependence between these two assumptions, each of which represents a side of the coin of confidence.

Up to the present time the question of confidence as it has been discussed by politicians and institutional leaders has tended to have a slightly negative quality in the sense that effort has been directed mainly towards the attempt to persuade foreign investors that they can proceed with confidence in Jamaica because nothing will happen to disturb their operations. We need to explore something more dynamic and positive than that. The confidence that we need to create is one which flows from within the local population and expresses itself in a faith in our ability to manage our environment and overcome our own difficulties. Not only is this the best guarantee of a nationally motivated economic thrust of a self-sustaining character but, curiously enough, is probably the best way of inspiring confidence in the external investor who observes us as an arena of opportunity with a critical and detached eye. Nothing commands confidence in others like confidence in one's self. Of course, confidence is an imponderable which cannot be turned on and off like a switch. On the other hand, if leaders can reach in to some inner reservoir of patriotic excitement and take pride in Jamaica's astonishing accomplishments in a huge range of human activity and, simultaneously, recognize that the doubts that linger were planted by history with no real root in present circumstances, I believe that a new and dynamic spirit can be released which will be self-generating, self-perpetuating and self-escalating. We must begin with an act of psychological disengagement: an act which Lincoln once described in a memorable phrase when he said to his own people: 'We must disenthrall ourselves'.

A parallel exercise of less specific significance but equal importance is to be found in the question of attitudes. Somehow there must emerge in Third World countries a commitment to excellence and an acceptance that work cannot be judged in terms of the stigma which were irrelevantly imposed as a by-product of slavery and colonialism. Martin Luther King once spoke of the importance of a man feeling impelled to be the best street cleaner in the world. With his orator's instinct for the illumination of truth by the personalized example, he put his finger on a problem which must be overcome. Interestingly enough, our progress is bedevilled not only by our unwillingness to perform supposedly unpleasant jobs, but by a more generalized malaise that extends to the whole business of performance. 'Time-serving' becomes the attitude towards work of any people who do not feel a specific connection between their degree of application to a task and the positive circumstances of their lives. The problem is exacerbated historically where colonialism created a generalized separation between the efforts of a people as a whole and the benefits which they derived from those efforts. Nor is this tendency to question whether effort is worthwhile peculiar to post-colonial peoples. One surely detects much the same thing with groups like the British worker whose experience of the Industrial Revolution and the early twentieth century culminated in the class disaster of the nineteen thirties and bred attitudes towards work performance with which the society continues to wrestle.

Insofar as attitudes are concerned, it is clear that leadership, exhortation and the force of example can play a part. In the last analysis, however, this kind of problem has got to be tackled at a completely fundamental level that recognizes every man's need to feel his importance in the scheme of things and his creative participation in the decision-making process. He must also believe in the connection between effort and reward and be confident that he is part of the social group which manipulates its environment as distinct from being a member of a *part* of the social group which is manipulated along with the environment by the *rest* of the social group. This last is the most fundamental transformation of all and the one that can most dramatically distinguish a man's view of his place in the environment of freedom from his experience of the environment of colonialism.

THE INTELLECTUAL EQUIPMENT

We must now turn from the psychological to the intellectual. The question of how a nation equips itself for the pursuit of its own objectives is now universally accepted as fundamental to all social engineering. With all the effort that was made in Jamaica between 1945 and 1972, the criticism remains that it was all too often a largely unthinking response. Having inherited from Britain an educational system already regarded as out of date in its country of origin, we proceeded with a strange blend of energy and innocence to its uncritical implementation. However, it is quite clear that other people's systems of education are unlikely to be capable of wholesale transplantation to any developing country. Nor is this an area in which we dare make a mistake. Education is the means by which we equip today's generation for tomorrow's possibilities. This demands a careful assessment of the kind of economic development of which we are capable, which is modified both by the opportunities and limitations of our physical environment and by a calculation of how these relate to national objectives. The educational system must seek to produce the skills which are a calculable part of our opportunities and the kinds of attitudes without which skills are sterile and the successful pursuit of objectives unlikely. This whole area is fundamental and is an indispensable key to development.

PLANNING

As we have indicated before, planning requires the focus of defined objectives. Hitherto, we have tended to regard economic growth as the sole purpose of planning. With our attention firmly focused upon things rather than people, it is not surprising that we have paid far more attention to the statistics of growth than to the figures of unemployment; nor is it, I suppose, surprising that the fact that unemployment grew faster than the economy seems to have occasioned little alarm. If, however, we accept that economic growth is not an objective in itself but a result to be desired to the extent that it creates the conditions within which to pursue full employment and a rising standard of living for everyone, then we have introduced an important new criterion against which to measure our planning options. Let us, therefore, bear constantly in mind our two prime objectives of full employment and the distribution of wealth designed to reduce the gap between rich and poor and achieve a kind of economic development that is general rather than exclusive in its impact. These objectives imply a number of things which I cannot hope to analyse exhaustively in this chapter. Let us, however, isolate four areas that are of obvious importance.

First, the area of research: all technological adaptation and, consequently, much economic development can be traced to research. But every country pursues research in terms of its own general, national or particular, sectoral needs. It is unlikely, therefore, that the research of one country can provide all the answers that are relevant to the needs of another. Therefore, developing nations must devote a substantial proportion of their resources to the development of their own research techniques and processes. In Jamaica very little attention has been paid to the research function. As a consequence, we have very little knowledge of the by-product possibilities of our own plant life or as they might be developed from the rich variety of fruit which are peculiar to ourselves. Equally, little attention has been given to market research aimed at finding answers to the problem of developing a demand for the wide range of exotic fruit and attractive woods which can be grown here. Having never explored market possibilities, we have not paid much attention to whether we could find ways to preserve our exotic perishables. Therefore, our planning cannot focus effectively upon new possibilities that we might discover for ourselves through the research process.

If we turn to planning itself we are faced with a second problem. Because of our chronic tendency to import other people's technology, we have condemned ourselves to the kind of capital intensive processes which are appropriate for metropolitan countries at their contemporary stage of development. But capital intensive technologies are not basically suited to a country like Jamaica. Planning, therefore, should focus upon the exploration of new technological 'mixes' that seek to find a balance between modern equipment, where this is necessary, and the maximum use of labour. The slavish employment of metropolitan technology will leave us with a mounting unemployment problem. Nor can we afford to turn the clock back indiscriminately. Therefore, we must press on to the evolution of a technological mixture that is our own.

Our third and fourth areas relate to inter-industry linkages and value added. Since we cannot afford to assume that unplanned growth can by itself supply the answers that we need, we must direct growth consciously. This involves identifying and isolating areas of by-product development, linkage development and the exploration of every possibility that increases the proportion of local value added to the total productive process. This implies in turn a willingness to commit government resources to the development of these areas or, at the very least, to create special conditions within these areas so as to ensure their exploration by the private sector.

Once again it will be observed that this kind of selective planning becomes a logical extension of national priorities once these have been identified. In the absence of such priorities, however, it becomes impossible to plan in this way since one is literally proceeding in the dark. As I have remarked before, there are no economic miracles. Survival is a matter of margins. The solution to unemployment and the distribution of wealth, therefore, lies in the fullest exploration of every marginal opportunity within a sharply focused system of priorites.

AGRICULTURE

Recent history has helped to persuade many observers that it is impossible to make a serious impact upon both the general state of the Jamaican economy and its capacity to distribute its benefits equitably if there is not a major assault upon the problems of agriculture. This is partly so because of the large proportion, perhaps 25 per cent, of the working population which depends directly upon the land for a living and partly because it is precisely in the failure of agriculture that we find a primary cause of the increasing gap between the rich and the poor in the society. Until very recently Jamaican agriculture had been surrendered by the society to what seemed like a permanent embrace of traditionalism. The export crop sector had totally failed to come to grips with the problem of modernization and no one had found an answer to the perennial problem of small farmer productivity.

I would suggest that Jamaican agriculture has to be seen in terms of three distinct challenges and possibilities. In the first place, the export sector must be modernized. But this will not occur if it remains in the hands of its traditional ownership, because there is not the entrepreneurial skill present to tackle the job and the pattern of ownership makes central planning impossible. Moreover, its recent record of performance has made it a kind of 'dead end' of the economy that is no longer capable of attracting private capital on the scale that is needed to do the job of modernization.

The key to the reorganization of the export crops such as sugar and bananas lies in rationalization and, certainly, in the case of sugar, the massive re-equipping of the processing side of the industry. To accomplish this it is necessary for the government to move into an active and dynamic partnership with the existing interest in the industry, first to secure the creation of a central institution through which effective planning can take place and, second, to ensure the introduction of top grade managerial and executive talent. Once this has been done one will find that it is possible to attract major capital through the international lending agencies for the purpose of re-equipping the factories, rationalizing transport and for the fullest exploration of by-product development. It may well be that many of the fears that now attach to any attempt at rationalization in the area of labour displacement will prove to have been exaggerated. An effective programme of by-product development may well absorb much of the labour that might be displaced by modernization. In addition, however, government's participation in any planning of this sort is the best guarantee of a rational programme that includes the accurate forecasting of labour displacement so that retraining programmes can be developed to fit displaced labour for other, expanding sectors of the economy. For years this exercise has been postponed, partly as a consequence of political resistance and finally, because the frustrations that were engendered eventually created an entrepreneurial malaise that reduced an already less than dynamic entrepreneurial group to a state of total paralysis. However, this adventure can no longer be postponed. The traditional export sector of the economy must

D

be made efficient so that it becomes a dynamic contributor to an expanding economy rather than an unofficial extension of unemployment relief.

The second main area of consideration is the small, largely hillside farmer. This group has been defeated by a combination of the smallness of his average holding and the difficulty of the terrain which he must farm. His present situation is not the result of any lack of markets. The food import bill of the Jamaican population has risen from $30 million in 1962 to $70 million in 1972. The problem is one of production not marketing opportunity. This is the area where the Jamaican Government and the farmer have got to recognize that they share a joint responsibility to use co-operative techniques to achieve economies of scale. Millions of dollars have been poured away over the years in trying to find various ways of helping the farmer to take advantage of this market. I suggest that all such methods will continue to fail because until he benefits from economies of scale it is impossible for the Jamaican farmer to take advantage of his opportunities.

This whole problem needs to be tackled in two ways. First of all the society must make up its mind to guarantee to purchase at remunerative prices everything that its farmers will produce provided this production falls within guidelines that are laid down by the planners. This is going to involve a substantial degree of political education and the development of radically different marketing techniques. However, it is idle to talk about balanced economic development if we are not willing to face what is involved. Simultaneously, so far as the farmer is concerned, he must be persuaded to cast off some of the individualism of the past and to be willing to combine with his neighbours for purposes of marketing and in relation to the sharing of modern equipment. Jamaicans often assume that our poor record with co-operatives means that there is some character flaw which inhibits progress in this direction. I think this is nonsense. Not enough effort has been devoted to the study of what has caused co-operatives to fail and as a result we have little idea about effective co-operative techniques in the Jamaica situation. The most difficult form of economic organization to maintain in viable production is the co-operative because it has no simple pyramid of authority to hold it together. Yet hours of study are lavished on how to make authoritarian productive units more efficient while we seem to imagine that the infinitely more difficult task of making a co-operative work is something that can be safely left to nature. What requires urgent attention, therefore, is the whole question of co-operative technique as it might be successfully adapted to Jamaican needs.

A third and virtually unexplored area which is of great significance to the future of Jamaican agriculture is a new type of export thrust. We have always assumed that the only two opportunities available to Jamaican agriculture are the home market and the traditional export crops like sugar. But with the increasing sophistication of the consumer markets of North American which are the hallmark of contemporary metropolitan economic patterns, a whole new arena of opportunity exists for the ingenious exporter. When one thinks of fruit like the ortanique, the naseberry, the Bombay mango, the avocado pear, it is not difficult to imagine the tremendous marketing opportunities that could exist if one could bring together skilful marketing techniques with a sustained production drive. What is needed, first of all, is the confidence to believe that we can do it and that we have products that could really excite the metropolitan palate. This is the sort of marginal addition to small farmer income that could revolutionize the capacity of Jamaican agriculture to provide an avenue to reasonable prosperity. But all of it is going to require a high degree of confidence, planning, ingenuity, determination, discipline and will.

Let us now consider the question of incentive and ownership. In all agricultural development it is vital to ensure that those who work the land have a stake in its product. Hence, any plan for sugar reorganization must, in my view, include immediate attention to the question of worker participation in ownership. It may well be that one needs to separate all farm operations from factory operations and find a means of bringing lands that were formerly owned by the factories under the ownership of farmers and workers who actually grow and reap sugar cane. Similarly, it is very important that present government programmes aimed at bringing thousands of idle acres into production as efficiently and rapidly as possible, should have as a long-term objective, experimentation in forms of ownership through which the people who develop these lands and who show a willingness to stay with them can come into various kinds of co-operative ownership. Later in this chapter I will consider in a more general way the implications to both the economy and the society of this kind of programme in both agriculture and industry.

A final question that needs to be considered in relation to Jamaican agriculture is the question of participation in owner-ship of secondary industries which are developed to take ad-vantage of agricultural production and its by-products. It is vital that we should continue, and develop to the level of a national policy, beginnings that have been made in, for example the coconut industry. In the case of coconuts, coconut growers not only grow and reap the crop but own the big factory that processes coconut products. In that way the grower not only retains a basic control over the wealth that is created by his product but also has the opportunity to share in later stages of 'value added' that arise subsequent to the reaping of the basic item. So long as the farmer is seen as a planter and reaper pure and simple, so long will he tend to be condemned to the low end of the 'value added' scale for exactly the same reasons that have condemned colonial territories to this end of the scale in comparison with metropolitan nations. The same factors that apply internationally apply within an economy as between the manufacturing and the agricultural sector with the same con-sequences. We are faced either with a process of legalized charity, which we dignify with the term 'subsidy', so as to maintain a balance between the earning power of the agricultural and in-dustrial sectors, or we must find a way to make the agricultural sector and the farmers who are its foundation, the beneficiaries of the more sophisticated processes that are increasingly derived from the basic activity of farming.

TOURISM

Looming large among the industries that need special thought is tourism. Few economic activities seem to occasion more extreme, and sometimes hysterical, comment than tourism. Rational analysis of this industry has been considerably obscured by two extreme and irrelevant points of view, both of which seem to owe more to an inferiority complex than to judgment. On the one hand, there are the protagonists of the industry who have contended that the road to success lies in the incarceration of the tourist in spectacular, multi-storied buildings built on top of white sand beaches within whose walls the tourist is encouraged to drink himself silly while remaining oblivious to the country beyond his hotel window. This school of thought seems to rest, at least in part, on the assumption that the rest of the country is an object of shame which the tourist could not possibly enjoy. At the other end of the scale are the opponents who see tourism as a form of organized mass prostitution and who are convinced that such social morals as survived the colonial experience will finally succumb to the corruption of the tourist dollar. It will be observed that this group shares with the first an equal lack of confidence in their own society. In fact we cannot afford to do without tourism. No industry grows as quickly in today's world, nor is as capable of rapid local expansion. In addition, it is one of the most labour intensive industries left to the modern world. Finally, it has a highly satisfactory multiplier effect when planned intelligently.

One must take certain basic factors into account when planning a tourist industry that can make a maximum contribution to economic development, in a manner consistent with national objectives. First of all, one must banish from one's mind the entire concept of the tourist. What one needs to develop is a vacation industry designed to cater not only for rich foreigners, but also for foreigners who are workers, foreigners who are black and, by no means least, for one's own local population. This means that one has to design one's facilities so that they cater for a number of economic levels and to create an atmosphere in which the visitor from abroad and the domestic holiday seeker feel that they have equal access to what is a truly attractive location. Second, it is vital that the vacation should not consist of imprisonment in a hotel. Rather the hotel should be the spring-board for the maximum involvement in the activities of the community. Art galleries, restaurants, night clubs, theatres should all be consciously developed in a vacation area so that the vacationer becomes involved in all that is most attractive in local culture. Equally, advantage should be taken of Jamaica's spec-tacular scenery to ensure that the vacation includes planned visits into the interior of the country where, in turn, restaurants and craft industries can all spring up as valuable additions to the economics of the interior. In this way the whole population will come increasingly to feel that it has a stake in the industry both from the economic point of view and in the sense that no quality of exclusivity behind high walls attaches to the vacationer. Finally, it is vital that planned programmes of urban renewal should be associated with and should take place in juxtaposition to hotel development. To put hotels beside slums is to provoke the occupants of the latter. To accompany hotel development with urban renewal is to present the slum dweller with tangible evidence that this development is in some way related to his own progress as a human being. When this kind of balance and planned approach is taken to tourism it will cease to be a source of tension and will become merely another highly rewarding aspect of the general adventure in economic progress.

BAUXITE

Jamaica's Bauxite industry[1] combines challenge with opportunity to an unusual degree. It represents the largest single capital investment, earns the most foreign exchange and pays the most

[1] SELECTED STATISTICS ON JAMAICA'S BAUXITE INDUSTRY

	1970	1971	1972
1. Bauxite mined (million tons)	11.8	12.2	12.3
2. Alumina processed (million tons)	1.8	1.9	2.0
3. Persons employed	13,390	11,629	9,719
mining and processing	5,493	6,162	6,756
agriculture	1,987	1,529	1,433
construction	5,910	3,938	1,530
4. Value of exports ($ million)	186.9	180.2	188.2
(as % of total taxation)	248.8	282.7	300.8
	(6.6)	(6.4)	(6.3)
5. Taxes and Royalties paid ($ million)	31.4	34.2	24.5
(as % of total taxation)	194.0	229.8	270.6
	(16.2)	(14.9)	(9.1)
6. Contribution to G D P ($ million)	137.9	134.5	129.3
(as % of G D P at factor cost)	(14.2)	(12.8)	(11.2)

7. Total Investment 1959–72 $550 million
8. Acreage owned at December 1969   191,000 (7% of total area of Jamaica)

    Acreage in mining etc.   14,000
    Acreage in agriculture   150,000
    (including forestry)
9. Number of Companies in Bauxite/Alumina Production   4 (1972)
    Number of Companies in Bauxite Production only   2 (1972)

taxes of any industry in the island. On the other hand, it employs a mere half of the work force currently engaged in tourism and about one-sixteenth of that employed in the sugar industry. It is exclusively under foreign ownership and control, processes less than a half of its mining output to the alumina stage of the aluminium process and has established no major aluminium fabricating complex in Jamaica. The industry has made an uneven contribution to agriculture with the tens of thousands of acres that it holds for mining purposes, has been slow to train nationals for management and makes a contribution to infrastructure that owes more to public relations techniques than a genuine intention to contribute to national development. In addition to all of this, the industry represents Jamaica's first major experience with that complex and controversial phenomenon of international economics, the multi-national corporation.

Because of its size and nature, the bauxite industry is best dealt with in the context of the discussion of foreign policy, foreign capital and how each relates to economic development.

FOREIGN AFFAIRS

It should be clear from much that has emerged in this chapter, and in particular our consideration of the problem of the terms of trade, that Third World economic development cannot be analyzed other than in the context of international affairs. Clearly, Third World countries must evolve a strategy in foreign affairs that reflects their common problems and needs. Such a strategy must take into account the terms of trade, the movement of international capital, the applicability of foreign technology, patterns of international trade, and the right of self-determination. All this must be seen in terms of a search for Third World self-reliance based upon a grasp of the similarity of Third World problems. In this context, the multi-national corporation is not the least of the challenges to be met. However, this area is too large to be dealt with in parenthesis and will form the subject of Chapter 3.

FOREIGN OWNERSHIP OF RESOURCES

It was Aneurin Bevan who coined the phrase 'the commanding heights' to describe those sections of a country's economy which are of strategic significance. It was a singularly felicitous phrase, particularly for any politician who is seeking to devise strategies of change. If we might borrow the phrase here, it would be true to say that 'the commanding heights' of the post-colonial Jamaican economy were, and are, almost exclusively in foreign hands. The entire bauxite and alumina industry is under exclusively foreign ownership. More than one half of the sugar industry, significant elements in the public utilities, the banking system, the insurance business and a substantial proportion of the burgeoning tourist industry were and are similarly situated. Clearly, political independence and national sovereignty are inconsistent with a situation in which 'the commanding heights' of the economy are foreign-owned and controlled. Indeed, throughout the Third World, this thesis has been massively and continuously argued, analyzed and documented. The issues that are involved are too well rehearsed to require repetition here. Suffice it to say, however, that I share the view that political independence and foreign economic domination of strategic sectors of the economy are mutually exclusive concepts.

Economic strategy must have as its short and medium range objective the devising of the means and institutions through which a developing nation can exercise *control* over the strategic sectors of its economy so as to ensure that these factors operate in a manner that is consistent with national objectives and planning. It means, further, that it must be at the very least a long-range objective to bring these sectors of the economy under local ownership of one sort or another. It must be borne in mind that these strategic objectives must be judged, in the Jamaican context, in the light of local reality. Here we are concerned with two issues: first, that foreign capital should be invested in areas of need and should pursue policies which are generally acceptable; and, second, that it should continue to flow into Jamaica at a rate that makes possible the attainment of the overall growth rates that the economy must achieve. Foreign private capital that is already here must certainly be involved in questions of control and general harmony with national objectives. New foreign capital, however, must be seen in two perspectives. On the one hand, it is a necessary part of economic strategy that foreign capital should be, to the greatest possible extent, public and institutional rather than private in character so as not to continue to add to the general problem. On the other hand, private foreign capital is still needed and welcome but should always be invited on the basis of joint venturing either with the public sector represented by the government or with the local private sector so as to ensure future harmony. Certainly, an immediate and urgent objective is to secure a situation in which no economic decisions affecting Jamaica are taken in foreign board rooms. This, of course, has considerable implications for the multi-national corporation.

All this comes more sharply into focus if we consider a number of basic issues that surround foreign capital in a developing country.

FOREIGN CAPITAL

Foreign capital, like tourism, tends to provoke strong feeling. Historically, the term evokes the worst recollections of colonial exploitation. Even in today's world overseas investors seem to be slow to learn the lessons of history. Even where the pressures of government and public opinion have forced them to conform to the standards of good corporate citizenship at home, they will revert to type in the more permissive atmosphere of some struggling economy abroad. One can often see reflected in the behaviour patterns of the foreign investor all of the moral bankruptcy of the early thinking which sought to justify the brutality of the Industrial Revolution. The world has paid a high price in human and social terms for whatever gains in productive efficiency can be attributed to the profit motive. By the same token we have paid our dues at the altar of the 'dictatorship of the proletariat'. On the other hand, we can learn a lot from the observation of both concepts at work and by an evaluation of the sheer human misery that has been visited upon mankind by the apostles of both.

In economic development, as with so much else, one must begin by ridding one's mind of the unconscious prejudices which are induced by the flood of propaganda that accompanies the unfolding of history. When we stand back from history in this way, it will become apparent that foreign capital is just another of the elements which go to make up the total equation of economic development.

Depending on how clearly we can identify our own objectives, foreign capital can make a significant contribution to the rate at which a developing country can overtake these objectives. In fact, it can be argued that no developing country can hope to bridge the gap between performance and expectation without substantial injections of overseas capital. Egypt could not have built the Aswan Dam, nor could the Castro regime have survived, without Russian capital and technology. Similarly, Jamaica could not have established her alumina industry by herself. Therefore, the question is not whether to use foreign capital in development planning. Rather, the question is how to bring foreign capital into harmony with national aspirations. In this regard, three prime considerations are: the purpose to which foreign capital is put; the price that one pays to put it there; and the extent to which national needs affect the decision-making process in the areas of its operation.

Insofar as areas of activity are concerned, there is obviously a negative side to this equation that presents no difficulty. Any nation can prevent foreign capital in a particular area by executive decision. For example, the government of Jamaica would not allow any foreign entrepreneur to establish casino gambling in Jamaica. On the other hand, one cannot order foreign capital to one's shores. Thus, having decided that it would be desirable for foreign capital to operate in a particular area, it is necessary to create the conditions in that area which will lead to a decision on the part of those who control foreign capital to invest. From this point of view, policy considerations are not unlike those which we have just described in relation to the general question of planning and priorities. Where foreign capital is concerned, however, one must look more closely at the question of whether one wishes the particular activity in the hands of private foreign capital or whether one might prefer to have the government borrow through one of the international lending agencies, so that the particular external capital is actually administered under local control. Decisions of this sort must stem from an assessment of the price which has to be paid for the capital and the technical skills which may become available through the capital. Hence, one may prefer to borrow capital from abroad because the level of profit that would be required by the private, foreign entrepreneur is higher than one would regard as consistent with the national interest. On the other hand, the profit expectation of the foreign entrepreneur may seem reasonable and he may have available to him an exclusive mastery of a particular technology which one may regard as important to the success of the outcome.

In terms of the price that has to be paid, the same sorts of factors have to be weighed. Here one must look at profit expectation in the case of privately controlled capital, as against the sort of rates of interest and sinking fund that would be involved in a foreign loan. Once again, it will be observed that the permutations and combinations of the problem are considerable and the choice of a solution, something that has to be considered on the merits of each situation.

Turning to the question of control, it is vital that this factor should be uppermost in the mind of the planner if the long-term interests of the nation are to be protected. One has a choice between three main devices. There are control mechanisms that can provide the rules within which foreign capital may operate in a particular area. There is nationalization and finally, there is the device of the joint venture which is a technique particularly suited to the circumstances of a country like Jamaica. Of course, torrents of words have flowed on the subjects of nationalization and expropriation of foreign capital. By nationalization, we mean the purchase of a foreign asset at a price that has been determined as fair by some impartial machinery provided by the law. By expropriation, we mean the seizure without compensation of a foreign asset. Of course, it is possible to acquire foreign assets on terms that fall somewhere between nationalization and expropriation. If, however, one is prevented by moral commitment and Constitution from following the path of expropriation, then one is left with a range of options that stop with nationalization. This is the case in Jamaica where nationalization arises because the terms on which foreign capital has entered the country in the past are not necessarily consistent with our concept of the national interest in the present. However, nationalization poses a number of problems, not the least of which is the question of the export of capital that is required to purchase the assets. It may well suit a country like Jamaica to deal with what one might describe as 'the foreign capital of the past' by the judicious use of control mechanisms. In this way one can secure policies that are broadly consistent with national objectives. On the other hand, it should be fundamental to future policy that foreign capital should enter on the basis of the joint venture. By this means one can secure local control of policy, the retention of a significant proportion of profits and the development of that national self-confidence that flows from a visible local presence in all major national undertakings.

OWNERSHIP

Let us now consider the whole question of the ownership of resources from both the point of view of the nation and of the individual citizen. Land is the basic resource of a people. It should never be out of national ownership or control. In a country like Jamaica we have inherited a situation in which a substantial proportion of our land is owned either by non-nationals or by nationals who have no desire to develop it. Ownership by non-nationals should never be permitted as a matter of principle. In the case of a small island like Jamaica struggling to support two million people, principle is reinforced by common sense since foreign ownership of our land not only mortgages our future but represents a current pressure on a scarce asset. Where land is already in non-national hands, there should, therefore, be the most careful set of rules concerning the use to which that land is put. Insofar as the future is concerned, land should be leased for specific development purposes, but never sold. By the same token, nationals who hold land for speculative purpose should be required to develop what they own immediately or sell it back to government.

Nor should this concept stop there. Apart from plots of land for purposes of building a home, the whole idea of private ownership of land is inconsistent with national economic planning in a context where it is assumed that the general social good is the objective towards which all effort must be directed. The past is littered with examples of land settlement schemes which were intended for agricultural production but where plots of land ended up being held for speculative purposes. When this happens it not only defeats the purpose of land reform, but increases the pressure on land room by withholding land from economic development. It should be standard policy to lease land in these circumstances and on conditions where the purposes to which the land may be put are clearly defined and the lease revocable in the event of default.

Another national asset that should never be in private hands and should, indeed, be available to all of the people all of the time are beaches. Although this proposition has almost universal acceptance, Jamaica has been slow to recognize the social implications of the question. As a consequence, we are only just beginning to wrestle with a problem that should never have been allowed to arise in the first place. A lot of our best beaches were sold to hotel interests in the days when we were willing to pay a higher price to attract the tourist than he was, in fact, demanding. This is a classic example where policy did not represent a measured response to reality but was determined, instead, by the insecurities that beset the post-colonial mind.

We now need to consider the ownership of the means of production from the point of view of the individual citizen. The capitalist system was first defined in a manner that suggested that there was a permanent and pre-determined distinction between he who owned capital and he who was employed on its behalf. The dividing line between the owner of capital and the worker was sharp and absolute. The decision-making process, the management function and an indefinite entitlement to the lion's share of the proceeds of economic activity were reserved to the owner of capital. Obedience and a subsistence wage, variously defined, were the lot of the worker.

Whole populations were brainwashed into believing that these distinctions were divinely ordained and represented immutable laws of the system itself. In fact, it was this assumption of immutability that misled Marx into assuming that the capitalist system would develop in a completely predictable way. As a result, he failed to allow for the possibility of capitalist adaptation and assumed that the system could only head for a sticky end. With corresponding inflexibility Marx predicted that ownership under the capitalist system would be concentrated in fewer and fewer hands as it headed for inevitable revolution. It is curious that so great a neo-Hegelian thinker should have failed to perceive that he, himself, would create a political antithesis to capitalism which would lead to a new historical synthesis.

In fact there was nothing immutable about either the laws which appeared to surround the capitalist system nor the divisions of functions that were traditionally associated with its workings. The decision-making process was attached to the ownership of capital because capital itself was scarce while labour was abundant. In addition, those who controlled capital had a virtual monopoly on knowledge. This was so because capitalism emerged at a time of elitist stratification of society where education was the exclusive preserve of the elite. Equally, the ownership and control of capital by a small minority of the society arose largely from the nature of society at that time and not from any logical historical force. Inevitably there have been very substantial modifications to the capitalist system that have emerged as society has evolved and as the economic system has grown more complex. For example, the decision-making process has been virtually taken out of the hands of those who own capital and is now to be found in the hands of the technocrats who run industry. This has occurred partly because economic activity has become so complex as to require an entire management class who are trained in what is a completely specialized area of knowledge. Also, the steady displacement of the old family business by the new corporate empires with their huge shareholding base has created a type of ownership that is too widespread to permit either group coherence or a sense of participation in decision-making. Of course, in the widening of the base of ownership through the development of the modern corporation, one can observe one of the significant adaptations of the capitalist system which have falsified the Marxist prediction of increasing concentrations of ownership and have given to the capitalist system an historical resilience which Marx did not foresee. In spite of these changes, however, there is still a characteristic tendency to assume that there is an enduring validity to the basic distinctions which existed at the start between owners of capital and workers. Certainly, in the post-colonial Carribbean these distinctions are fundamental to the existing social order.

One major reaction to the manifest injustice of these functional distinctions within the capitalist system is to be found in the communist model of state ownership. In this model there is no distinction between owners and workers and so, to that extent, one can point to a theoretical gain in terms of egalitarianism. However, both models have, in my view, proved to be unsatisfactory. One does not need to elaborate upon the inadequacies of the capitalist model with its built-in master-servant imperatives. But the state industry model as it emerged in Russia is just as deficient from a number of points of view. This model is authoritarian and subject to control by the Party and its representatives to the exclusion of effective worker participation in decision-making. In terms of the workers' day to day experience the egalitarian advance is, therefore, illusory.

If one wishes to experiment with models of ownership and patterns of human relationships within industry one must, I suggest, begin with the individual, the nature of man and the areas within which he seeks satisfaction. I suggest that there are two clear needs which must be met if the average man is to maximize his satisfaction as a working member of the social group. First, he must feel that he has a stake in the economic activity to which he sets his hand. Second, he needs to feel that he can influence his environment. These imply in turn that each man engaged in an enterprise should feel that he has some share in its ownership and stands to benefit directly from the wealth that it creates. Also, there is the implication for the decision-making process: each man should feel that he can, if he wishes, make a contribution to the processes by which decisions are arrived at. In the classical capitalist model, the worker has neither a stake nor access to decision-making. Similarly, neither of these things is necessarily present in a state industry. I contend that if we are to attempt a social order that is rooted in egalitariansim and a notion of justice, our economic organization must be designed to satisfy these two needs of 'stake' and 'participation in decision-making'. It is only when these two conditions are present that we can claim to have made our economic arrangements a part of a satisfactory system of social relationships.

There is, however, more to the question of the worker's role in industry than the satisfaction of theories of social justice. I believe that it is only by this route that one can guarantee in the long run both peace and efficiency in industry. The world is trapped in a contradiction with grave implications for the future. Both in the capitalist West and in most of the communist East we are trying to maintain a system of economic authoritarianism in the face of an educational system that increasingly produces a conscious, highly trained and articulate human being. At the same time our political systems proclaim the freedom of man and the primacy of his rights. As a consequence our educational system and our political ideals combine to produce a kind of man who increasingly expects to be a force not only in his political and social environment but also in that most fundamental of all his spheres of experience – his working life. Nor is this idle theoretical speculation. Anyone who has compared the difference between the attitude towards authority and discipline in a plant on the part of older workers who grew up accepting yesterday's assumptions, with younger workers who are the products of the new educational and political forces of the world, is struck by the latter's impatience with things that the former takes for granted. This is not happening by accident but is the living proof of the proposition that we are educating the world beyond the possibility of a continued acceptance of any kind of authoritarianism – and economic authoritarianism is no exception.

We cannot turn back; therefore we must press forward, accepting fully the implications for social and economic organization of the forces which are liberated by modern education and politics. This can only be done if we accept the implication of the training which we make available to our citizens and understand that training does not only increase skill and adaptability. It also increases both the expectation and the capacity to make a contribution at the decision-making level. Nor can we continue to assume the kind of man who is content to suffer on a picket line periodically to extract an increase in wages. More and more the modern world is bound to create the kind of man who will ask: Why should I have to fight for a share of the product which should be mine by virtue of the fact that my skill is an indispensable input? The alternative to the conscious development of a system that rests upon worker ownership and participation will be mounting industrial tension of a kind which the conventional union movement will be increasingly unable to accommodate within its traditional spheres of action. It is going to call for highly sophisticated strategies and institutional techniques of new kinds to effect the kind of transformation in the system of ownership that is envisaged. Among other things there will have to be a very substantial process of education about new economic relationships since many who express the kinds of aggressions that are the product of the contradictions within which they are trapped, do not yet perceive either the source of their frustration nor its remedy. But this need not be a cause for discouragement. Rather it is one of the great challenges to the social ingenuity of countries in the Third World. After all, we come to the problem with the peculiar advantage of being the heirs to a historical commitment to change and are happily free of any national responsibility for the development of the various patterns of economic authoritarianism.

If we can achieve such a social order one can be sure that the system of ownership that would result would ensure a far more equitable distribution of the society's wealth. General participation in the decision-making process would help to make each citizen feel that he or she had a creative contribution to make to the economic process. And it is probable that productivity and discipline would benefit from the general atmosphere of involvement. Certainly, we can be sure that the present pattern which seeks to guarantee discipline through the capacity to apply sanctions is headed for diminishing returns. We live, after all, in a world that is increasingly populated by human beings whose needs for creative engagement increases as the boundaries of knowledge expand. Increasingly, discipline will prove to be a function of involvement and understanding rather than of fear.

CO-OPERATIVES

While new techniques are explored in the area of worker ownership, the role of co-operative organization needs radical re-examination. The co-operative is the institution best able to accommodate the needs of both economic and social strategies. It is the means by which the economies of scale can be placed at the service of the small man without sacrificing his stake in ownership. In the Jamaican situation it is the form of organization that could solve the problem of small farmer efficiency. Co-operative technique would permit skilled artisans to group themselves together in organizations which could play a significant part in the development of the service sector of the economy. Through co-operatives, the consumer could introduce a new dimension into the distributive sector.

Ironically, Jamaicans have been chary of co-operatives, pointing to a high mortality rate in the attempts that have been made. In an argument that represents a triumph of whimsy over investigation, it is contended that Jamaicans are individualistic by nature and therefore lack that capacity for self-discipline which is the foundation of a successful co-operative. All that this really means is that co-operatives in Jamaica have been badly organized, badly managed and ill-understood by those who were involved in their operation.

The co-operative form of organization requires very strong management of a highly specialized kind. An ordinary business enterprise under the capitalist system requires management that understands the logistics of production and marketing together with the techniques of money management that keeps these two considerations in proper relationship. However, the relationship between the human component and the organization exists within an authoritarian frame and, though calling for sophisticated management, rests ultimately upon a simple truth. Implied in the relationship between the organization and the people who work for it, is the capacity of the former to apply sanctions to the latter. As a consequence, performance is subject to discipline.

By contrast, the co-operative involves a coming together of sovereign equals. The organization that results enjoys no separate status of authority and must, accordingly, depend upon continuing consent. In this situation, the capacity of the group to maintain a disciplined relationship must proceed from an entirely different kind of management in which persuasive communication must take the place of the sanctions which are available to an authoritarian organization.

Interestingly enough, in the few co-operatives which have been successful in Jamaica, we find that great emphasis was placed on leadership and communication. What is urgently required here is an intensive investigation of co-operatives that failed. The lessons that are learnt would prove invaluable in the development of techniques of co-operative organization and management. Such an exercise is critical to the development of a strategy in regard to co-operative organization which, in turn, is an important element in the search for economic democracy.

RURAL DEVELOPMENT

Any reasonably balanced economic development must take into account a number of special factors. First of all, resources must be allocated so as to ensure adequate rural development and the commitment of capital to the provision of infrastructure and industry so as to create the basis for a balanced and satisfactory life for rural dwellers. Planning must take into account the quality of rural life as well as the necessity for a viable rural economic base. Without both economic viability and a quality of life commensurate with modern expectations, the hope of developing strong rural communities will be stillborn. At present rural communities in Jamaica are places where old men get ready to die and from which the young flee in search of contemporary dreams. This process must be reversed. Of course Jamaica is no exception to a general problem throughout the developing world in this regard. A companion exercise in Jamaica's case, however, is the necessity to develop major urban alternatives to the capital, Kingston. At present Kingston and its suburbs contain nearly one third of the Jamaican population (600,000 out of two million). The capital is already experiencing the big-city problem of unmanageability. Jamaica needs to plan the conscious development of a least two other major urban centres. These should be Mandeville, which is beautifully situated in the mountains in the middle of the island, and is almost at the point of the centre of gravity of the bauxite and alumina industry. The second should be Montego Bay, the tourist capital, which is on the north-west coastline and should develop logically into the urban focus for western development.

GROWTH

Economic growth is important but not an end in itself. Indeed, growth statistics can be hopelessly misleading. For example, the period in which alumina plants are built in an economy on the Jamaican scale, create an illusion of considerable growth. In human terms, however, these plants may represent a minor employment factor and may actually occasion a period of reduced tax earnings for the economy. This occurs since capital allowances have traditionally led to large write-offs in the early years of the life of an alumina plant by comparison with the comparatively handsome royalties that would be earned on bauxite mining. If economic growth is intended to be the servant of a just society, planning must be discriminating and keep constantly in mind the human equation. Economic activity which reduces unemployment, and is planned so as to create the opportunity for meaningful economic participation for people, contributes to personal happiness and, therefore, to justice. But growth does not, of itself, guarantee these things. Growth must, therefore, be the subject of unceasing scrutiny so as to ensure that it enlarges the creative scope of the society and leads to a more just distribution of its benefits. In the past, for example, undiscriminating reliance upon growth saw the emergence of the 'two-tiered' economy which led to increasing imbalances in the distribution of wealth.

However, it remains critical to maintain a rapid rate of economic growth. While this commands a general consensus, it is not always understood that growth itself depends upon more than the management of internal market and investment factors. Critical as these undoubtedly are, it must be borne in mind that growth is often stifled by an unwillingness to think beyond traditional factors. For example, dependence upon traditional markets is a major limiting factor upon growth. Jamaica must see the world's markets as a stage upon which she must seek her self-interest with ingenuity and infinite flexibility. Hence, growth itself, which the layman often assumes is the exclusive concern of the economist, the entrepreneur and the sector planner is, in reality, dependent on a total strategy which ranges from the climate of attitudes, through the development of human skills and includes a foreign policy which is geared to every shift in the winds of economic opportunity around the globe.

INCOMES AND DISTRIBUTION

Jamaica along with every other society in the world which claims concern about social justice, must face the issue of an incomes policy. In the context of a free society this is proving to be the most difficult of all the strategic requirements of social justice. Incomes policies have been bedevilled by controversies about prices, profits, comparative wages and the mutual distrust of all the elements of the society which might be affected by restraints in the national interest. And yet we cannot hope to fashion an egalitarian society if we do not face the issue of rationality in the rewards for effort and the distribution of wealth. In terms of economic planning, a broad national consensus over an incomes policy is a pre-condition both of orderly development and of the hope for a society resting upon the just distribution of wealth. Undoubtedly, this issue strains to the limit the capacity of a free society to agree upon policy. But if freedom is to be the condition in which justice flourishes the issue must be faced and overcome.

Clearly, success in the development of an 'incomes' policy is intimately linked to the control of the factors in the distributive system which affect prices and the cost of living generally. So long as the less affluent suspect that the price of a loaf of bread may include an unreasonable profit margin somewhere along the line, it will prove difficult to gain acceptance for the idea of rationally ordered incomes. This is, therefore, an area into which the government must move. It is true that price controls are difficult to administer and harder to police. However, the effort must be made because far larger issues depend upon the attempt. Certainly, a government must take responsibility for the purchasing of the raw materials upon which the staple diet is based. Commodities like wheat, corn, soya beans, rice and the like cannot be purchased in circumstances where doubt may attach to whether the cheapest source of supply is involved. Nor is it fair to ask the private sector to disregard its traditional relationships and to accept the cheapness of the source as the sole criterion by which it is to be guided. Only a government is capable of that freedom of action.

Simultaneously, goverment control of the basic marketing mechanism in these fields permits flexible planning of agricultural development geared to import substitution. The protection of the consumer can be married to the development of productive capability within a rational framework that guarantees public confidence in the outcome as measured by prices.

One other factor which may influence attitudes towards an

incomes policy is the degree of organization attained in the field of social security. The elements of social welfare in terms of pensions, protection in illness, care for the handicapped and the like are so fundamental to social justice and have been so often discussed, described and analyzed as to require no repetition here. Suffice it to say that the concept of security from the cradle to the grave is fundamental to social justice. Indeed, it is implied in the very fact of social organization and was probably its primary purpose at the time of *Genesis*. Where people feel secure in their ability to cope with illness, injury, old age, the education of their children, they are more likely to take a rational view of their incomes in relation to society's needs.

AN ECONOMIC PROFILE

No examination of the problems of the Jamaican economy would be complete without an attempt to paint a picture of the sort of economic structure towards which we should work. In attempting to draw this economic profile one is by no means suggesting a structure for all time. Rather, we are seeking to indicate a structure towards which we can work realistically within the constraints to which we are subject at this time in our own history and in the world context which we occupy. What we will seek to do is to consider 'the commanding heights' to which we alluded earlier, the manufacturing sector, the farming sector and the distributive sector and consider these in relation to public ownership, foreign private ownership and local private ownership.

Broadly speaking, we identified 'the commanding heights' as those sections of the economy which occupy a strategic position. Hence, the public utilities, the banking system, the bauxite industry and the sugar industry can be said to constitute the principal elements in 'the commanding heights' of the Jamaican economy. These quite clearly belong in public ownership and control. As a matter of common sense and reality, public ownership will have to work together with foreign and local private capital in some areas in the foreseeable future. For example, the bauxite industry would be best organized in Jamaica in joint ownership between the government of Jamaica and the private corporations. The latter control the markets and have access to capital and technology on the scale that we need for major development of this industry which must include aluminium smelting, the establishment of a fabricating complex and the development of linked input industries such as caustic soda and the starch which is used as a flocculent in the alumina process. Hence, this mixture of public and private foreign capital is likely to be the logical pattern for the bauxite industry in Jamaica in the foreseeable future.

In the public utilities, on the other hand, it should be possible to evolve a situation of complete public ownership with reasonable speed. The sugar industry lends itself naturally to joint ownership between the public sector, private local capital, foreign local capital and local farmer interests. In this mixture the public and local farmer interests should ideally predominate. This sort of mixture between the public sector and foreign and local private capital seems ideally suited for the banking system provided the local interest predominates. The decision-making process should be carried out locally by Jamaican nationals and the whole system should be under government control insofar as basic banking policy is concerned. The same pattern should obtain with other financial institutions such as insurance companies. Here is it worth noting that public institutions such as the Development Bank, the Mortgage Bank, and the Workers Bank all have critical parts to play in development strategy and it is vital that they should be linked with the commercial banks to ensure the fullest collaboration between the public and the private sectors in the pursuit of national objectives.

Throughout the whole of these strategic areas of the economy, the element of public ownership is important not only to ensure harmony with national policies but also as the means of ensuring the genuine democratisation of ownership in Jamaica. It is socially important that all these industries should reflect a substantial measure of worker ownership and should be organized on the basis that all those who work in these industries should have a voice in the decision-making process. This kind of public sector participation is a critical element in the development of techniques and institutions through which there can be a growing transfer of ownership into the hands of the employees, at all levels, who run these vital industries and economic institutions. The only possible exception to this general rule is in the case of the public utilities. It may not be in the public interest to seek to run a public utility on a profit making basis and therefore worker ownership may in this context, invite a conflict of interest. It could be that the consumer co-operative would be the ideal method of ownership for certain types of utilities. However, these detailed questions can be resolved in each case once a clear concept is accepted.

The ordinary manufacturing sector belongs naturally in private hands. However, it is vital to the development of the kind of society which we envisage that there should be a growing local, small businessman sector to manufacturing industry. Just as it is vital to pursue a deliberate policy of worker participation in ownership at all levels of the economy, so is it vital to create the institutions which can assist in the rapid development of the small operator in the manufacturing field. This can involve a wide range of activities such as furniture-making, laundering, maintenance services and workshops, tailoring and dress-making establishments and so on. It should be a matter of deliberate policy to keep the economy from becoming cartelized. The best way of ensuring this is to create the institutions which can help the small business element to be efficient and competitive. This may even involve the conscious creation and maintenance of co-operatives among small manufacturers as a means of maintaining the balance between themselves and the highly organized, large scale enterprises.

The real fields for co-operative development, however, are the distributive trades and, of course, farming. The development of consumer co-operatives in the distributive industry is an important element in a just economic order. Furthermore, it is not necessary for the whole of the distributive industry to be in the hands of consumer co-operatives so long as the sector reflects a reasonable proportion of this kind of organization. Once consumer co-operatives exist in sufficient numbers and in strategic geographical locations, they can act as effective monitors on the performance of the distributive trade. In any event they represent an important step forward in the whole process of economic participation. Co-operative ownership is, after all, an important aspect of the strategy by which one must attempt consciously to create an economy that is owned by the people in the widest possible sense.

It is in agriculture, however, that the co-operative movement has the largest part to play. Co-operative ownership of farming is the critical means by which agriculture can be developed on the kind of scale that permits efficiency, through organization in optimum units, while at the same time retaining the element of personal ownership. It is also necessary to see the farmer in relation to what he produces in much the same way as one sees the worker. We have argued that the worker is entitled to a share in the ownership of the enterprise for which he works because his labour represents an input which is just as critical as capital. Once he shares in ownership, he shares automatically in the wealth which his product generates. Similarly, we must see the farmer as the producer of a commodity which is not only sold in its first, raw state, but which is also often developed through processing and the manufacture of by-products. Hence our argument that the farmer must become a beneficiary of the 'value added' which is created in succeeding stages of the development of his primary crop. This will require the reorganization of the relationship between farming and agro-industry.

Beginning with co-operative organization at the farm level, we need to create structures of ownership which lock the original co-operative into a share of the ownership of the succeeding stages of economic development, based on the original crop. In this way one can make farmer and workers alike share naturally in the general growth of the economy and ensure that they share proportionately in the national wealth that is created at various stages. Only thus can we solve permanently the two problems that have bedevilled every economy in the world: that the wealth of the farm sector does not keep pace with that of the manufacturing sector; and the worker has to fight for a fair share in both sectors. Some societies have tried to solve these problems by the legalized charity of subsidies on the one hand, and militant unionism on the other. A method of more enduring validity would be to devise the institutions through which the farmer can share automatically in the wealth that is created by the processing and general utilisation of his crop, and the worker share automatically in the fruit of his hands.

Thus we see the picture of an economy with a public, a private, a small business and a co-operative sector. We see a clear place for foreign and local private capital. We also see a principle of widely based citizen participation in ownership in the private sector along with the principle of worker participation in ownership throughout the public sector and in all the reaches of 'the commanding heights' of the economy. We see the farmer and the small businessman retaining the 'feel' of ownership in a co-operative form of organization which simultaneously guarantees the economies of scale. In this way small unit ownership can be allied to large unit efficiency. We see the development of consumer co-operatives and institutions such as workers banks and management advisory services to small businesses. We must make available to every citizen in every walk of life and reach of the economy, the kinds of services that have hitherto been the exclusive preserve of the more favoured sectors of the economy. In short, we see a participatory system which has as its ultimate objective the concept that every single citizen should own a part of the economy and feel, as a consequence, that they are genuine part-owners of the nation.

3

Foreign Policy

FOREIGN policy begins with the perception of self-interest. In the metropolitan countries foreign policy is regarded as an automatic and critical element in government strategy. The combination of size, economic power and sheer experience which are a part of the situation of a metropolitan nation leaves its people in no doubts as to the importance and relevance of this aspect of government. This comprehension is harder to come by in the case of a newly independent territory particularly if that territory lacks either size or major economic significance or both.

In any event the reality of the colonial experience is likely to have left in its wake a failure to appreciate that a country's relations with the rest of the world can be as important to its development as the relationship between the various parts of itself within its own territorial boundaries.

In the case of a country like Jamaica we find all three disabilities (geographical, economic and perceptional) present to an unusual degree. Jamaica is small. Apart from its bauxite industry its disappearance from the world scene would create scarcely a ripple on the total surface of the world's economic relationships. Finally, our experience with colonialism went on for so long as to create a near paralysis of judgement in the area of external relationships. As a consequence it has taken Jamaica quite a period of time in the immediate post-independence period to begin to appreciate all that is involved in its external relations. Long habituated to trade with Great Britain, the United States and Canada, the average Jamaican even at the start of the decade of the 1970s found it difficult to comprehend the possibility of a relationship between Jamaica and the rest of the world. This is so despite the fact that communist Russia has long been our best customer for pimento and despite the fact that we recognised communist Yugoslavia shortly after independence. These were disconnected, one might almost say disembodied, events which

123

seemed to hang suspended in the midst of a general assumption that the real world began in Miami from whence it proceeded due north to Canada swinging vaguely eastwards through Newfoundland but ending irrevocably at a line that might be drawn between London and Edinburgh.

It is obviously important for Jamaica to retain its friendship with this part of the world and if possible to extend and deepen its economic relations with the United States, Canada and Great Britain. However, the perpetuation of dependence upon these three relationships is inimical to Jamaica's long-term interests and is only favoured by those who remain frozen in the postures of yesterday.

Jamaica is a part of the Third World. By the Third World one means that entire range of countries, mainly tropical, that were the scene of the great colonial explosion which reached its crescendo in the latter part of the nineteenth and the first part of the twentieth centuries. All of these territories stretching as they do through the Caribbean, Africa, India and the Near and Far East were used as sources of raw materials and primary agricultural products destined for the great manufacturing centres which were mainly concentrated in Europe. After the Second World War a reverse political process commenced led by India and quickly to be followed in the Caribbean, Africa and the rest of the colonial world. In short order all the former colonies had attained political independence. However, without exception, these territories entered upon political independence suffering from enormous economic disabilities.

We live in a world of instant communication. This ensures that, in a manner never experienced by mankind before, both standards of living and the ideas that attach to them experienced in one part of the world become part of the consciousness and, thus, the immediate aspirations of everyone else in the world. As a consequence, implicit in the popular support for political independence is the notion that independence should confer upon the newly liberated people the economic benefits and standards enjoyed by their former colonial masters. However, the basic economic equations which were left behind as the colonial tide receded made these popular aspirations impossible of early satisfaction. As is now well understood, all the newly independent territories have found themselves trapped in an economic dilemma. Their trade is established in traditional patterns with the metropolitan powers. In these patterns, the former colonies supply the basic materials which attract the smallest share of the 'value added' of the total economic process. These are exported to our metropolitan partners and in return we import the manufactured goods and the products of heavy industry which represent the lion's share of the 'value added' of the total process. To begin with there is this disequilibrium between what the former colonies have to offer and what our metropolitan partners supply. To make matters worse the prices of raw materials and primary agricultural products show an historic tendency to instability around general levels that do not tend to rise. On the other hand, the prices of manufactured goods in world trade tend to be consistent within a pattern of steady increases. As a consequence, and as is well documented, it takes more and more tons of Jamaican sugar to purchase an American or British tractor as the years pass. Hence, the terms of trade which are inherently against us to begin with, tend to move increasingly against us.

Finally, the former colonial territories entered upon their independence desperately short of capital and of the means to accumulate capital for themselves at a rate consistent with the consumer standards which their people had come to expect. As a result, it is vital that these territories should be able to attract overseas capital. However, we find ourselves once again in a dilemma because the price of money and hence the terms on which capital is available moves steadily to our disadvantage. So all these territories share a common dilemma of high expectations, disadvantageous trade and insufficient capital which it is increasingly expensive to attract.

A country like Jamaica cannot begin to formulate a foreign policy until it understands its place in relation to this general world problem. Since the Second World War Jamaica has sought to solve its problems by assuming, as a constant of policy, that the United States, Canada and Great Britain represented the total horizon of our opportunities. Hence it was felt that insofar as there was a foreign policy at all, it consisted of seeking favours from these countries in the form of economic aid and special price supports for certain products like sugar, bananas and citrus. The combination of this foreign policy together with a certain view of economic strategy, which we examined in the last chapter, had brought us by the 1970s to the totally unsatisfactory situation which we sought to analyze.

Where results are the opposite of intentions it behoves a man to re-examine his strategies. Let us therefore begin by taking a fresh look at a foreign policy for a country like Jamaica.

The first thing that we have to appreciate is that in economic terms size is increasingly a pre-condition of survival in the world. Hence a first thrust of foreign policy for a small country must be to seek to become part of a larger economic region which provides a larger basic market together with greater opportunities for economic specialisation. Once this is grasped it is not too difficult to move to the second leg of a foreign policy which flows from the recognition of the common dilemma of the Third World.

In Jamaica's case the break-up in 1961 of the abortive West Indian Federation created a general ambivalence towards regionalism even in its economic form. It is *not* the purpose of this book to debate the issue of political Federation which is closed for the time being. It *is* the purpose of this book, however, to point out that the emotional consequence of the political trauma of 1961 must never be allowed to cloud our judgement of contemporary reality. It is vital to Jamaica's future that we should play our part in the creation of a Caribbean Common Market[1]. This involves many steps and considerable technical adaptation but the objective must be clear and must be of an eventual scope to include all the countries of the Caribbean regardless of their ethnic, linguistic or political characteristics. Indeed, in the broadest sweep of history, economic regionalism must be seen as extending to include all the countries of Central and Latin America which embrace the Caribbean. Guyana and Belize represent geographical out-posts and are historical pioneers of this concept. Belize, Guatemala, Honduras, El

[1] The Treaty establishing the Caribbean Common Market was signed at Chaguaramas, Port of Spain, Trinidad, on 4th July, 1973. The date, which is the anniversary of the birthday of the Jamaican National Hero, the late Right Excellent Norman Washington Manley, was chosen as a tribute to his contribution to Caribbean Regionalism. The location was chosen as a similar tribute to the Prime Minister of Trinidad and Tobago, Doctor the Right Honourable Eric Williams.
Signing were Barbados, Trinidad and Tobago, Guyana and Jamaica. The author signed on behalf of Jamaica.

Salvador, Nicaragua, Costa Rica, Panama, Colombia, Venezuela, Guyana, Surinam, French Guiana and Brazil all form a natural economic region bounded by Barbados to the east and stretching up through Cuba, the Bahamas to Bermuda to the north. Geography and a shared colonial history combine with the characteristics of Third World underdevelopment to create a region that is just beginning to awaken to the fact that it shares a common, manifest destiny. This grouping contains the resources, the diversity and the scale of potential market to make it one of the viable and exciting development areas of the world. Furthermore, if its people can summon the historical vision and political common sense to move beyond the apparent ideological differences within the region, they could demonstrate to the rest of the world a new approach to the question of foreign investment. The Caribbean contains capital exporting countries like Venezuela as well as a number of nations which must still seek to import foreign capital and technology. However, all the countries of the region have suffered from exploitation at the hands of foreign capital and are, therefore, well placed to learn the lessons of history and to evolve new relationships in which the movement of capital is responsive to the needs and national objectives of both the exporting and the host countries.

The challenge of the future is to shake off the shackles of yesterday's assumptions which have delivered us into a separatist trap. The logic of tomorrow's possibilities unfolds in the larger context of regional co-operation and economic integration. This is so for precisely the same reasons that make it logical for the countries of Europe, after two thousand years of conflict, to form an economic block now. It is so for the same reasons that connect the respective economic accomplishments of America and Russia to their sheer size.

The perception that leads one to the conclusion that economic regionalism is a logical pre-condition of accelerated national development must now be applied to the world situation. It is one of the tragedies of the post-colonial period of all those countries which we now loosely describe as the Third World, that they have permitted themselves the luxury of ideological distraction. Quarrelling constantly about political matters, they have been woefully slow to appreciate their common economic dilemma and the importance that attaches to the development of a global

Third World economic strategy. Since every Third World country is faced with the same dilemma in its dealings with the metropolitan world it follows that Third World countries need to develop a unified response to these problems. Here it is my belief that one must begin with the principle of self-reliance. Consequently the first element of a Third World strategy must be the exploration of every single possibility of trade as between Third World countries. Every act of trade within the Third World reduces the general dependence upon metropolitan economic power. This is a largely unexplored area of considerable potential. But it is an area that will only be explored if Third World countries have the will and the determination to bring together their collective expertise to the study of trading possibilities between themselves.

Second, it is critical that the Third World should create its own institutions for savings and development. In addition we must develop policies of investment in projects that reflect Third World priorities. It is also important that Third World countries begin to exchange information about technology since, as we discussed in relation to economic planning, their own technological discoveries are often more likely to be relevant to each other's problems than the discoveries of more advanced nations. Thus beginning with Caribbean regionalism, a Jamaican foreign policy must be Third World in its economic orientation.

Finally, a foreign policy must recognise that we must, to a certain extent, continue to import capital and know-how from the metropolitan world. Despite the greatest application of internal, regional and Third World self-reliance this will continue to be so for some time. However, this must involve an 'open' foreign policy as distinct from the 'closed' policy of the past which only envisaged relations with our traditional partners. In this way our capital can be sought from a variety of sources and on a wide range of terms. This is an important insurance against foreign domination which is far more likely where the sources of foreign capital are concentrated in one quarter.

Of course, implied in the idea of Third World trade and indeed in the whole concept of an 'open' foreign policy is the matter of trading with countries whose ideologies and political systems differ from one's own. Because of the sheer inexperience of the world which is produced by colonialism there are many

Jamaicans who imagine that an exchange of goods in trade involves a rubbing-off of political taint. Obviously this is nonsense. Trading with communist countries, for example, does not import communist ideology into Jamaica nor for that matter does trade with Spain import Spanish fascism. All countries that are involved in trade do so from the posture of their own political systems and it is a betrayal of national self-interest to fail to seek out in the world at large those points of advantage to one's own economy. However, a distinction must be drawn at this point. One may refuse to trade with a particular country not because exchange might imply the transmission of a taint, but to exert diplomatic pressure. Hence, Jamaica does not trade with South Africa, Rhodesia or Portugal as a protest against apartheid, political repression and colonialism. In each case the policy involves the rights of a subject people and is, therefore, an appropriate target for international sanctions.

As I have indicated, trade between Third World countries is to be desired in itself because it reduces the incidence of something else that is working to our disadvantage. But even in our relationships with the metropolitan world it is fatal to believe that one's self-interest can be successfully pursued in one limited arena. There have been times in history for example, when America, Canada and Great Britain between them represented a disproportionate percentage of the world's economic power. These were the great capital exporting nations. And so our dependence upon them in the past may have been supported by a temporary historical logic. Today, however, the situation has changed. The United States and Great Britain both suffer from currencies that are under heavy pressure in the period of the 1970s and are no longer basically capital-exporting countries. On the other hand, there are countries in Europe and half-way across the world there is Japan which are the capital-exporting countries of today. A foreign policy that ignores this fact is unnecessarily limited with respect to its available options.

Obviously, if one needs to import capital and technology one must search in the areas where there is the disposition to export these commodities. In the context of an open foreign policy these options are available. Where the foreign policy is closed one may not even notice the new arena of opportunity.

Naturally, changes in foreign policy in a country like Jamaica

E

are yet another example of things that disturb the collective unconscious in its uneasy slumber. But these things must be faced.
The old way is disturbed so that the path to new opportunities
may be opened. In all this Jamaica has, it is my firm conviction,
a historic mission to fulfil. Our present circumstances place us
firmly in the Third World. Our historical conditioning has
fashioned us an essentially tough-minded and pragmatic mould.
Surely, therefore, we are capable of the emotional adaptation to a
Third World commitment to a new world order. I am equally
confident that we are sufficiently adept, by experience, in the
ways of the economic world to bring a cool pragmatism to bear
upon Third World passions so that these may be guided into a
constructive pattern of economic action and co-operation without
which the dream of those who were dispossessed can never be
brought to fulfilment.

In another context when we talk of an open foreign policy we
are seeking to establish the fact that the entire world is the
stage upon which a country, however small, pursues this perception of self-interest. Nor does one have to conclude that self-
interest is either an immoral or an amoral phenomenon. National
self-interest for example, leads no wise man into war. War has
often been the resort of fools like Mussolini or knaves like Hitler.
They shared a common fate. And even successful wars of aggres-
sion set in train forces that undo the temporary advantage that
they may confer. The only wars that are morally justified in
history are those dedicated to national liberation where it is clear
that no other method can succeed. Therefore a policy of en-
lightened self-interest will commend to any intelligently-led
nation the conclusion that peace is in every man's interest in the
end. Hence every country, and Third World countries even more
so, has a tremendous investment in the success of the United
Nations. But even as a supporter of the United Nations, it is
also important that our foreign policy reflect a clear adherence to
principle and the expression of those principles in the councils of
the United Nations. Very often international problems are so
tangled as to render the detection of a principle extremely
difficult. The commitment, however, must be there. One can
illustrate the difficulty by two examples, one of which represents
a case of obvious clarity and the other a case of perplexing
difficulty.

On the one hand a country like Jamaica must be totally dedicated to the active support of all those measures that can lead to the overthrow of the apartheid regime in South Africa, the Smith regime in Rhodesia and the Portuguese tyranny in Angola and Mozambique. In other words, where wars of liberation for the purpose of establishing national freedom are being fought, the objective of freedom legitimises them and commands our unswerving support.

On the other hand, if we take the case of terrorism we see a completely different picture. If terrorism is defined in a manner that includes African wars of liberation it is very difficult to see how one can oppose it. However, terrorism in the sense of hijacking planes, the slaughter at the Munich Olympics and indeed all acts that seek to involve innocent third parties as a means of applying pressure to an enemy represent outrages against humanity which are intolerable. The problem is how to distinguish the legitimate from the rest. One might retort that there is no situation in which violence can be justified at all. I am instinctively passivist and intellectually a part of the non-violent tradition of Ghandi and Martin Luther King. However, where one is faced with a tyranny like that of South Africa, one is forced to concede that there is not the remotest possibility that non-violent methods would lead to either the overthrow of that regime or even its substantial modification.

Can one, therefore, say that the black African does not have the moral right to resort to arms in the pursuit of freedom? And which metropolitan nation would dare to deny this right? The commitment must be to principle but tempered with a cautious recognition that many of the issues of international politics bristle with difficulty. In fact, it is the very complexity of these problems and the tensions that they create in the world that makes it so imperative that the United Nations itself survive and increase in influence and strength in the world. Hence a foreign policy must include a concern for everything that affects peace in the world which in turn implies a constant vigilance about international relations generally.

A relevant foreign policy for Jamaica might, then, be summarized as involving a positive commitment to Caribbean economic regionalism; the search for a common Third World economic strategy; support for the United Nations; unswerving commitment to the right of self-determination for small countries; support for policies that seek to express a commitment to international morality as distinct from cold assessments of self-interest in the context of world power politics; and an 'open' concept in which Jamaica seeks to maintain its traditional friendships while reaching out for the widest possible creative contacts in the economic and cultural field[1].

Within the framework of such a broad policy one has got to consider the problem of the multi-national corporation which, as we pointed out earlier, represents the most recent and complex expression of the problem of foreign capital in international affairs. A multi-national corporation is, of course, a single company which operates different aspects of a total industrial process in different parts of the world. For example, in the case of the aluminium industry, you can find a single company with headquarters, say, in the United States of America which may mine bauxite in Jamaica, Surinam, Australia, parts of Africa and the United States itself. Its alumina operations may be conducted in any or all of these countries. Its aluminum smelting will be sited predominantly in the United States but it may have smelters in one or two other countries. The extrusion and fabricating processes will again certainly be heavily concentrated in the United States but there may also be plants in some of the countries where one or more of the other operations take place; or it may have fabricating operations in some completely different country. Thus, with our decision-making process concentrated in one country like the United States of America, such a corporation will operate important aspects of its total business in a number of other countries.

As a consequence of this diversification of activity, the multi-national corporation is peculiarly insensitive to social and political control because no one segment of its business is concentrated in a sufficiently large measure within one area of political jurisdiction. Political decisions in relation to its operations tend to have very slight impact on its total economic operation and can, therefore, be far more readily ignored than would be the case if the

[1]For a full examination of Jamaica's position in relation to Caribbean Regionalism, see 'Overcoming Insularity in Jamaica' by the author published in the American Quarterly *Foreign Affairs* in the October edition, 1970.

whole or a large part of its operations fell within the focus of a single political jurisdiction. Of course, its headquarters are always located in the metropolitan power of origin, but that is precisely where there is least likely to be exerted the kind of political pressure in the realm of policy that would be likely to be consistent with the needs and interest of some far away, developing nation. Hence, its greatest point of vulnerability is also that point where it is least likely to be subject to social pressure. On the other hand, it is in the small developing countries, where its operations may have a substantial impact on the welfare of the particular nation and where, therefore, there is the greatest need for social and political control, that it is least vulnerable to pressure and the hardest to control.

It is not possible to conceive of an answer to the multi-national corporation outside of the context of international political co-operation. Interestingly enough, the workers movement, in its dealings with the multi-national corporation, has long since recognised the importance of co-operation. Realising that single unions trying to tackle one limb of the multi-national 'animal' would be up against disproportionate bargaining power, the international trade union movement embarked sometime ago on a studied policy of international union co-operation so that it could begin to match the bargaining power which, in the case of the multi-national corporation, can only be measured in international terms. Equally, Third World nations faced with this problem are going to discover that their most effective response to this phenomenon lies in practical co-operation between governments that are involved. The world has already seen a striking example of what can be accomplished at this level in the operations of OPEC. Through international action, oil producing countries have had a striking success in terms of prices for crude oil and in the area of internationally accepted levels of taxation and profit sharing in their dealings with the oil companies. Sources of primary ore such as bauxite and other metals are going to have to travel the same route if they hope for a similar success. Of course, there are difficulties inherent in the situation which are not easy to overcome. For example, bauxite exporting countries will be substantially affected in their struggle by Australian attitudes now that Australia has arrived on the aluminum scene as a major source of bauxite ore. Obviously,

Australian co-operation would enormously facilitate progress since it would represent a significant addition to the bargaining power of the group. But even if particular countries will not co-operate, the rest must take up the challenge because a start has to be made somewhere.

It must also be understood that this problem cannot be seen exclusively in terms of prices for basic ore. Effective policies in relation to multi-national corporations have got to take into account the entire range of processes that go to make up the total industry and must consciously seek to secure that secondary and tertiary processes are located within the Third World along-side the basic mining processes which are the first stage of a particular industrial process. Policies should also be evolved aimed at securing a reasonable measure of contribution by multi-national corporations to the development of vital infrastructure.

In short, the presence of the basic minerals which are needed for the metropolitan industrial process should be used by the Third World as a whole, as a means to securing a basic con-tribution to the development of wealth. In addition, these re-sources should be used as the spring-board for the planned development of the entire complex of industries which are associated with the basic resource. Finally, resource development must be associated with the creation of the infrastructure which is needed to support the sophisticated economic linkages that are involved. Furthermore, this kind of approach should not be pursued apologetically as if one were seeking metropolitan favours. Rather, it should be seen in the same clear-eyed, businesslike way as the metropolitan economic interests view Third World resources. The metropolitan operation is unsenti-mental and explicitly designed to obtain the most ore at the least possible cost – and without apology. Equally, we must plan to secure that we trade the least ore for the most benefit and must realise that in this context, benefit has a number of sophisticated ramifications and does not end with ore prices and royalties alone.

To succeed, a policy in relation to basic resources requires the rapid development of a considerable expertise to ensure that Third World countries really understand the capital, market, technological, transport and other implications of the various industries that are involved. Coupled with expertise, there must be Third World unity if policies of this kind are to succeed. Obviously, unless one Third World country happens to be in a very powerful position as a supplier of a particular raw material, it will find that it is in danger of being isolated when it attempts to bargain alone. If the Third World as a whole, however, establishes a policy of industrial groupings evolving joint policies and maintaining joint pressure within the context of general Third World political support, bargaining power will be enormously enhanced and progress facilitated. Once again, it is important that this kind of Third World initiative should not founder on any ideological rocks. The nationalisation of particular assets is only one aspect of a possible total strategy. At a given point of time some countries may wish to pursue this particular aspect to further their own national interest and others may not. What is important is that the Third World should not fracture its capacity for a generally unified strategy on account of particular differences in this regard.

One of the practical issues with which Third World countries must grapple in the immediate future is how to create permanent institutions that are capable of formulating specific proposals in these areas such as the relationship with multi-national corporations, questions of trade, exchange of technological information and development finance. The great problem is that the Third World has so far proven itself stronger in the realm of ideology and rhetoric than in formulating specific programmes of action. It is to this latter exercise that we are now summoned by our circumstances.

And it is here precisely that the Caribbean can make a tremendous contribution to the Third World and, indeed, that Jamaica can make a tremendous contribution to the Caribbean and, through its natural region, to the larger community. Caribbean man, if one may be forgiven the term, is the product of almost unique historical forces. The element of total transplanting together with an equally total absence of an historically indigenous population yet all joined in the bitter equation of colonialism, has created a people who are not quite like any other. If we could discover the key to self-confidence, we would find that our true strengths outweigh our weaknesses and that these strengths are not necessarily in over supply in the post-colonial world. It would be true to say that the Jamaican citizen is not naturally at home in the world of ideas and that political ideas are no exception. He is, on the other hand, a person of enormous adaptability and blessed with a rugged, humorous pragmatism which gives him a remarkable capacity for resilient survival. I choose the word 'resilient' because it imports a sense of readiness for progress. There are people in history who have responded to suffering with such bitterness that they succumb to a kind of smouldering anger which makes them destructive in outlook. There are also people who invest ideas with such passion that they become hysterically incapable of constructive action. In this regard, the world looks askance while the Irish wage a hot and brutal war ostensibly around an issue that should surely be *passé* by now. But somehow it is difficult to imagine a Jamaican reducing himself to progressive impotence in the name of a sectarian squabble. Somehow, he would cool the religious passion with humorous insight and leave his energies free to cope with the more practical exigencies of providing for his family. Hence, compared with many others the Jamaican personality may be less likely to trigger a heroic novel but is more likely to be involved in an economic miracle.

Beginning with his natural gifts of resilience and pragmatism, Caribbean man has demonstrated formidable prowess in the field of economic adaptation and political action. Colonialism left him with the negative legacies of an uncertain sense of identity, uneasiness in the world of ideas and an often unattractive appetite for conspicuous consumption. But it also left him with positive strength in the areas of political and economic action and in the mastery of the professions. The Caribbean, therefore, can serve as a bridge between the more extreme forces of the developed and the developing world. The role involves a constant summons to economic co-operation amongst developing nations. Equally, it involves the development of a persuasive diplomacy from growing strength aimed at the great economic powers. This policy must seek co-operation in the construction of a new world economic order based upon the concept of equity in the distribution of the world's wealth.

Sharing the situation and the experience of the former colonial peoples yet adept in the ways of the colonisers, the Caribbean can contribute greatly to the capacity of the Third World to translate ideas into action and to the possibility that the metropolitan world will modify traditional courses of action by the acceptance of new ideas.

Sooner or later the entire world must face this challenge of a new world order. Whole generations are emerging in both the metropolitan and the Third World that have been conditioned by the incessant preachings about international brotherhood, peace and goodwill. Increasingly the power brokers whose propaganda machines churn out this message of love while pursuing national self-interest with the most studied cynicism, are under critical scrutiny. Just as the forces of education are creating a man who will no longer accept the cruel simplicities of economic authority, so too is this same man increasingly questioning the credibility of the world power establishments. The process by which cynicism in the use of power in international affairs is modified is slow and painful; but slowly and surely progress can be observed. It may be that one cannot always attribute progress to enlightenment. Often, what appears to be progress is merely the discovery that the crude pursuit of self-interest can be self-defeating. But even if the lessons are learned in a negative way, a slow process of modification is taking place nevertheless. Furthermore, it is probable that metropolitan conduct will respond more quickly in the face of Third World unity where that unity expresses itself in practical action and is the beneficiary of calm and lucid articulation in the councils of the world. The Caribbean can make a significant contribution to both sides of the equation and can, in the process, help to accelerate the positive circumstances of its own progress.

4

Education

EVERY developing society must aim at free, compulsory, universal education as its highest national priority. However, considerable analysis of the educational process is required if the enormous effort that this objective implies is to prove worthwhile.

Education is normally thought of as the process by which the formalised knowledge of a society is passed on to its young through institutions of learning of one sort or another. It has, however, a wider connotation implying all the means by which the young are prepared for the adult experience and, indeed, the young and not so young equipped to play their part in society. It is in this wider sense that I wish to consider education in a developing country. Obviously, for a country like Jamaica education is crucial since every aspect of our society reflects the failure to achieve a harmony between aspiration and performance or even between the existence of resources and their use. For us, therefore, it is not enough that education should transmit our accumulated knowledge and skill from one generation to the next because most of our difficulties can be traced to the inadequacy of our skills and the misdirection of our knowledge. Accordingly education cannot be neutral; the educational process cannot consist of mere techniques for transmitting knowledge. If we are to attempt to overtake our expectations and engage our resources we must transform both the focus of our attitudes and the nature of our skills. Hence education is the key to what must be an act of self-transformation.

Right at the outset it is necessary to clarify a philosophical question about education which cannot be left unanswered. There is a view of education which seems to imply that the process must be restricted to the passing on of specific knowledge. In this concept the question of attitudes is deemed to be outside of the scope of the system. It is felt that attitudes are a private matter beween parents and children to be dealt with in the home and nowhere else. In this view of education, the nearest that a school would come to the business of attitudes would be in simple matters like discipline and good manners: and even here it is doubtful whether the emphasis on training in these areas reflects a desire to fit a young person for survival in the adult economy so much as the self-interest of the school itself which needs discipline if its lessons are to be heard and good manners if the pedagogue's life is to be endurable. Of course, this concept of education grew out of the great libertarian political movements whose primary motivation was resistance to tyranny. Jamaica imported its educational system from England and did so at a time when British education was, perhaps, the supreme example in the world of that view of education that restricts the process to absolute moral neutrality.

I can recall my own years at school as providing not one single course or class which was designed to give me an attitude about anything. The structure of the language, the dates of Nelson's victories, the laws of motion and the properties of a metal were taught with varying degrees of energy and skill, but no one asked me to consider whether there was any reason why I should be my brother's keeper or he mine. Social responsibility, government, political method or public morality were not even words to be wondered at because the school provided no books in which these questions were examined. Presumably these exercises were to take place at home. The great fallacy here, of course, lies in the fact that a father who has never been taught to consider these questions is not likely to discuss them with his sons. On the other hand, it must be recognised that many countries which have experimented with a more adventurous form of education, involving the conscious attempt to inculcate attitudes, have done so in the pursuit of dubious objectives. The political systems in which this has been tried have been, in the main, totalitarian. Here the State has usually sought to condition the young citizen to obedience coupled with a carefully nurtured acceptance of some central idea. One has only to think of the Hitler Youth Movement and the careful canvassing of the idea of a master race in the German educational system under Hitler to make the point. Unhappily, the idea of an educational process with a clear moral thrust has been gravely compromised by the totalitarian experience.

On the basis of this analysis it might seem that the choice lies between an educational system which transmits skills and abstract knowledge but which is morally neutral and socially unfocused, on the one hand; and a system which seeks to enslave a man's mind so as to ensure his obedience to the dictates of the state. The choice, however, does not lie between these two extremes nor is it even bounded by the categories which they imply.

Every educational system in history has reflected the interpretation placed by each society upon its own needs. Some societies may be slow to detect changes in the pattern of need and, hence, may cling to educational systems and processes that have outlived their usefulness. Other societies may suffer a temporary subversion of the educational process by a group who seize power because of a temporary failure of the political system. But these are historical aberrations. Basically, each society tends to use its educational system to promote its view of its own possibilities. In some societies possibility is bounded by yesterday's accomplishments. In this event, education will be conservative and may actually seek to inhibit change by a system of taboos. Education in a tribal situation has something of this quality because most tribal experience represents a moment of historical equilibrium and is, as a consequence, essentially conservative. In the same way, nineteenth century England represented an uneasy balance of power between a declining monarchy, a landed aristocracy, a professional middle class and a rising entrepreneurial class. It may well be that a neutral educational system represented a perfect compromise for the uneasy protagonists in such a situation. It may even be that the compromise was unconscious. Then again, a militaristic Germany in search of more land could logically be expected to supply the rationalisation for its ambitions through the concept of the master race and to ensure popular commitment through the educational process.

In the last analysis, therefore, each society fashions its response to the environmental challenge through the educational process. It is unrealistic to imagine that there is any conflict between neutral and positive educational systems to be resolved. What is needed is for the issue itself to be stripped of confusing irrelevance so that we can consider the question: How does Jamaica really view its own possibilities, and how can its educational system assist in their realisation?

Let us look at the question of skills first of all. To begin with the Jamaican educational system does not reflect a realistic balance between the needs of economic development and the actual training that is provided. The system offers courses that reflect the social prejudices which we have inherited from the past and bear little relationship to the kind of economy which we must seek to build. In the past, the economy was seen as a place which provided two alternatives. Either one belonged to the great majority who could not escape from the world of manual labour; or one belonged to the minority who enjoyed a privileged status through professional training or as a result of a minor excursion into the lower reaches of a classical education. In a sense this meant that the very skilful youngster could hope to become a doctor or a lawyer; the less skilful offspring would make it to the Civil Service and the least skilful would become a store clerk. This entire group comprised the middle class and were, of course, careful to restrict the educational opportunities which flow naturally from an academic education to members of the group. Of course, over and above the lower and middle classes were the land owners whose offspring were assured a prominent place in the economy whether they were educated or not. Since exposure to learning had little to do with the final position in society of this group, it had little influence on the educational system one way or the other. So far as the mass of the people was concerned, the most that it was thought necessary to provide by way of education was a very elementary form of the 'three Rs'.

Thus, the traditional pattern of education exactly reflected the realities of power within the system. The hereditary rights of the big land owners made education irrelevant; the professional, bureaucratic and clerical needs of a colonial economy were supplied by the middle class who were content with a system based on the English public school of the late nineteenth century; and the three Rs which were made available to some of the children of the masses exactly reflected the latter's position in the social and economic ladder.

If one chooses to forget the massive injustice involved in this system at the upper and lower ends of the scale, one can at least say of it that it was enough to keep the wheels of a colonial economy turning. However, an independent nation grappling with the forces of material expectation which are released by the drive for political freedom must build an economy equal to its appetite. This involves a range of human skills completely beyond the scope of anything that is involved in a colonial economy. It might be said, as a consequence, that the pre-condition of economic expansion in the condition of political freedom is the development within the society of the skills without which a sophisticated economy cannot function. Our educational system, on the other hand, has responded to the new challenge by seeking to expand the system in its old form. This has implied a considerable commitment of resources to provide more and more training, for a greater proportion of the youth of the country, of the same kind as heretofore. Thus, our educational system in common with the systems of many other countries in the Third World is in danger of producing increasing numbers of people fitted for the professions, the bureaucracy or white-collar careers.

Clearly what is needed is the recognition that the manpower needs of a modern economy are radically different from those of a colonial economy. If we are, on the one hand, to provide for ourselves the skills to build such an economy, and, on the other, to train a population that can find employment and economic satisfaction we must begin with a radical restructuring of the training content of the system. Architects, engineers of all types, cost accountants, statisticians, computer analysts, radiologists, research scientists, soil chemists, agronomists, farm managers, business administrators: these are the kinds of skilled personnel indispensable to a modern economy. Therefore, before even thinking of expanding available school plant, one should consider what kinds of early education will best prepare an adequate supply in these areas. This in turn leads to the question: How does the country develop teaching resources in terms of instructors, text books and the like, equal to these new demands? A failure to plan at this level lands a developing society in the middle of a dilemma. Either it is incapable of economic development or it becomes increasingly dependent upon imported manpower which is capable of operating at these levels. Therefore, the first educational response to freedom must be made in the area of technological adaptation.

This, however, has more than purely technical implications. It means that one has not only to plan consciously to provide a wider range of subject options for children, with all the technical adaptation that this demands within the educational process; but it also means that a way must be found to persuade children to choose new careers which are alien to the common experience. This last is more difficult than might appear on the surface because the traditional educational options leading to a traditional profession as the ultimate in opportunity are profoundly associated with status in the popular mind. Hence, the thought of becoming an attorney-at-law and a Queen's Counsel may seem far more attractive to the young aspirant than the prospect of a dubious odyssey into the locally uncharted seas of cybernetics. But if the society is to grow and if a rate of economic development is to be achieved that is even remotely consistent with popular expectations the means must be found to persuade enough young people to forget the study of the law and take up one of the new careers. Society cannot afford to wait for market forces to produce the required shift in the focus of personal ambition. It may take a generation before a sufficient number of personal economic failures due to an over-supply of lawyers teaches its lesson to the young. Thus it is obvious that the system itself cannot respond adequately by a mere extension of course options. A conscious effort to fashion new attitudes towards the educational process, its purposes and possible benefits is a necessary and parallel exercise. This in turn implies the development of an attitude towards society itself, its needs and the relationship between the individual and society. Hence, it is impossible to talk about economic transformation without accomplishing a transformation in attitudes. Political freedom without economic transformation is a contradiction in terms. Therefore, political freedom demands educational transformation aimed at both technical adaptation and new attitudinal patterns.

Before looking at the question of attitudes and education, however, one additional implication in the area of formal education must be examined. Granted that the educational system of a post-colonial society must seek to train in new areas of skill, it must also beware of a danger that is inherent in that exercise. It is inevitable that the teaching of new skills should begin with a relatively simple process of importation and imitation. In the areas which I sought to indicate by the examples mentioned earlier, there is a body of knowledge in the world at large which is objective and relevant regardless of environment or circumstance. However, the young country must be constantly on its guard against the uncritical importation of technology which may be relevant in a highly sophisticated metropolitan economy but may be counter-productive with regard to the stage of economic development of an emerging nation struggling with its peculiar social problems. Hence, a modern engineering course may teach, with exemplary logic and relevance for a metropolitan context, the value of modern heavy equipment in road building. But exclusive reliance on these techniques may be disastrous in some young countries which may be wrestling simultaneously with unemployment and a balance of payments problem. Local manual labour may well be the logical response to both problems. Curiously enough this problem is often discussed by planners but consideration of its implications has not yet found its way into the Jamaican educational system because of the uncritical importation of its various components.

An even more important area of concern is the question: How does a society like Jamaica develop the innovative spirit? How does it develop both the specialist skills that are necessary for the research process and the self-confident, questing attitude that are necessary for the innovative spirit and the research process alike? A part of the answer is, of course, technical in the sense that it is influenced by the organization of the latter stages of the educational process and by the degree to which resources are committed to research purposes. There is reason to suspect, however, that performance in these areas is as much influenced by attitudes as techniques. Here one can see yet another example of the impossibility of distinguishing between technical and moral categories as they relate to the question, what should education seek to achieve in a developing society? Obviously, a developing society will not develop a by-product technology without purely technical skills. On the other hand it will not put its technical skills to work in the search for by-products if there is not a kind of attitude prevalent in the society which has the self-confidence to believe that it can find new answers for itself; nor will it consider the search worthwhile in the absence of a general faith in the future of society together with a commitment to the idea of a national adventure.

And so we come, as we must, to the question of attitudes in a post-colonial society and the role of the educational system in the general task of psychological transformation.

As always, we must begin by defining our objectives. I suggest that we can distinguish four clear areas. First it is important to seek to instil a spirit of self-confidence individually and collectively, so that the psychological foundation for self-reliance may be laid. Second, one must consciously train young people to accept the spirit of social co-operation as the foundation of national success and achievement and as a natural result of social and political awareness. Then one must strive consciously to create a general acceptance of the work ethic as both a means to personal satisfaction and the personal investment that each man must make in the progress to which he is committed by his ambition. Finally one must seek to train people to be capable of self-perception. It is only through the awareness of the self in its relationship to the social group and, hence, of the social group in relation to its total environment that one can hope to create the psychological climate within which self-confidence, a spirit of co-operation and the acceptance of work as a creative aspect of experience are possible for a people.

Before considering some of the specific difficulties with which we must deal, and possible educational strategies to deal with them, it might be useful to make a general comment on the relationship between culture and self-confidence in a post-colonial society.

Clearly, no search for a strategy likely to induce national self-confidence can proceed without an awareness of the cultural implications of our situation. The term 'culture' is often misunderstood as suggesting the refined aesthetic sensibilities of the elite; hence terms like: 'he is a cultured man' or 'he lacks culture'. This, however, represents the petty conceits by which an elite bolsters its courage. For the purposes of this discussion, I am using the term in its wider sense in which it implies all the means with which a society expresses itself. Many thinkers have spoken of the effect of colonialism upon a people's culture. Obviously as we indicated before, colonialism represents a period of cultural strangulation which arrests a natural social evolution.

An inevitable by-product of this process is a reduction in self-confidence. Therefore, post-colonial societies must accomplish two things if they are to re-establish self-confidence and re-embark upon the process of self-discovery that is expressed by the evolution of a people's culture. They must rediscover the validity of their own culture at the moment of the colonial intervention and retrace the steps that had led through history to that point. And they must establish within a frame of reality, the culture which colonialism imposed upon them so that this may loom neither larger nor smaller than it deserves and suffer from none of the distortions which can result from the ambivalence of a ruler-subject situation.

There was a time when Jamaican poets spoke of daffodils and snow neither of which are noticeably a part of the Jamaican scene. Since 1938, however, our sculptors, painters, novelists, dramatists and poets have become increasingly the mirrors through which Jamaica can see herself. This has led to an art movement that combines vigour of expression with relevance of comment. In the context of an egalitarian concern, it is fascinating to note that the artists themselves have sprung from every walk of life and share a remarkable *camaraderie* and community of interest. During the 1960s the field of popular music which used to be completely derivative, ranging from adaptations of *The Mikado* to an almost stupifying appetite for exact renditions of the songs, styles and variations of leading American pop singers, has shown hopeful signs of indigenous vigour. Urban poverty has at last asserted its own reality and troubadours of ghetto misery, frustration and hope have emerged. The search for self-confidence demands the organization of training, economic opportunity and constant mass exposure for all these artists so that a total dialogue with the society can be assured.

In all this, however, there remains an aspect of our cultural situation about which the average Jamaican is confused. This is the question of Africa and its place in our past, present and future. I remarked earlier that all post-colonial societies must re-connect the threads that lead from today through the colonial trauma to the past. For many English-speaking Caribbean nations, this is difficult because colonialism spanned for us, some three centuries and because slavery added a dimension to the Caribbean situation that has no parallel in the colonial experience

of Africa, India, Indo-China and the like. Our form of slavery
meant that ninety per cent of our people trace their historically
recorded, and hence conscious, origins to slavery itself. Among
other things, this geographically transplanted institution was
designed to destroy all cultural links with the past. The threads
of which we spoke are frayed, not only by colonialism, but by
slavery. The consequence of this is seen in a deep confusion in
the pattern of Jamaican attitudes towards race and towards
Africa. At the slightest provocation, Jamaicans of the deepest
hue will hasten to assure you that 'you can't trust black man'.
Others are uneasily convinced that Africa is the home of the
'Bongo man'. Still others will implore you with pathetic sincerity
to 'leave all this Africa business alone'. At the opposite end of
the spectrum there are those who cannot accept the negativism
of shame. Struck by the contradiction between white symbolism
in a land of black skins, they take refuge in an opposite irration-
ality, declaring that God is black and that they want to 'go home
to Africa'. Between these extremes lies a path of sanity. (God,
naturally, is multi-hued; and each man must make his land his
home).

It is pointless to either over-rate or under-rate the accomplishments of Western civilization. It has produced dazzling technology and a persistent capacity for self-destruction. It has produced the most articulate philosophy in recorded history and a
rapidly dissolving moral foundation for social organization. It
has produced spectacular productive capacity and a chronic inability to share the benefits of production equitably. It has produced societies that encompass within the range of their contributions to history – Beethoven and Goethe on the one hand,
and Auschwitz and Dachau on the other. Clearly, there is no
cause for alarm and hysteria here. The good and the evil, the
success and the failures, are nicely balanced, and compare neither
favourably nor unfavourably with any other human experience.
However, to the average Jamaican, and I suspect others of the
English-speaking Caribbean, the African side of our heritage is
shrouded in mystery and covered with shame. Few are conscious
of the fact that much pre-colonial African social organization
made the European nation state look like an aggregation of
blood-thirsty barbarians. Few have the objectivity to recognise
that African tribal wars, before and since colonialism are only

distinguishable from their European counterparts by the fact that
metropolitan technology increased the European death toll. Even
fewer realise that African art is perhaps the only inspiration that
stands between many European artists and a final surrender to
abstract decadence.

If people are to acquire self-confidence and rediscover the
cultural continuity to which they are heirs, the mask of obscurity
and shame must be ripped from the face of our African heritage.
Once again, this will disturb the establishment, but it is a pre-
condition of national maturity. Cultural exchanges between the
Caribbean and Africa and the introduction of a stream of basic
teaching about African history must take their place alongside the
flow of European artists who are understandably encouraged by
the British Council and similar metropolitan bodies. If we are
to know ourselves, we should know at least as much about the
Ashanti wars as about the Wars of the Roses. If we do not know
ourselves, we cannot hope to acquire the self-confidence upon
which the spirit of self-reliance must rest.

We now need to look more closely at what precisely we mean
by self-confidence. Perhaps this is best accomplished by specific
examples. A people may be said to possess self-confidence when
they take it for granted that they have the capacity within the
resources of their own collective intelligence and skill to find the
answers to their external environmental challenges and their internal social difficulties. I would not doubt that it was the
recognition that an earlier America had possessed this quality
that led Kennedy to challenge America with the concept of the
'new frontier'. It is clear that he hoped to precipitate a new mood
of national self-confidence by invoking the memory of the past.
By contrast, that same America entered the 1970s so entangled in
the futility of Vietnam and frustrated by the problem of the
unmanageability of the modern city that clear signs were developing that suggested a crisis of confidence. Americans were
literally losing faith in their capacity to respond to external and
internal challenges. However, this doubtless represented a
temporary and perhaps superficial phase in the American experience. By contrast, the problem with a post-colonial society
like Jamaica's, is that its people do not necessarily begin with the
positive assumptions that are implicit in national self-confidence.
As I remarked earlier, the post-colonial citizen begins by doubt-

ing his capacity to influence his external environment and, faced
with internal problems seeks refuge in someone else's expertise.

How, then, can an educational system strike at this problem
and release in a new generation the creative energy which is the
ultimate expression of self-confidence?

Obviously, there are no simple answers to the problem of
developing self-confidence through education. Confidence, as
distinct from its lack, is a relative thing. There is a sense in
which the mere act of learning something will in itself tend to
create self-confidence. Equally, there are members of post-
colonial societies who have been extraordinarily successful in
mastering the conventional educational disciplines and yet have
emerged from the experience totally lacking in confidence as we
have just defined it. Obviously, therefore, we are dealing with a
state of mind that involves three distinct levels: the acquisition
of knowledge itself, the development of the innovative or en-
quiring spirit, and the question of identity. Each of these has a
bearing on self-confidence and in turn, is affected by the presence
or absence of self-confidence. Clearly, then, an educational
strategy must bear all these categories and their interdependence
constantly in mind.

Beginning with knowledge itself, this must be taught, not by
rote but by techniques that relate knowledge to the capacity to
perform effectively through its application. This is generally
recognised as important by modern educators but takes on a
peculiar urgency in developing societies beset by their peculiar
difficulties.

Conscious efforts must be made to build into the system of
education every device and technique that contributes to development of the spirit of enquiry. Practical problems should be posed
to children individually and in groups so that they learn at the
earliest age to accept the analysis of problems and the fashioning
of solutions as natural to the human condition. Once again this
is neither revolutionary nor new in terms of educational thinking,
but must be seen from the standpoint of the transformation of a
society to whom these things do not come naturally.

Insofar as a sense of identity is concerned, every resource of
ingenuity should be directed towards the teaching of things that
create a sense of being part of the historical continuum which
we discussed earlier. We will discuss aspects of this a little later

but note, in the meantime, that even the techniques for transmitting knowledge can be used to instil a sense of national identity and confidence. Mathematical problems for example, can be expressed in terms that relate to immediate personal experience and can be so devised as to invite solutions that contribute to an atmosphere of confidence. I have often wondered, in this connection, why a mathematical problem must be expressed, say, in term of two trains travelling at different speeds and the time which one takes to come upon the other. Exactly the same lesson could be taught in terms of the number of people who need to be taught to read and write in one country and how long it would take to accomplish total literacy if one mobilised a certain number of voluntary teachers for the purpose. A comparison made with a neighbouring country which mobilises more teachers and gets to the objective of total literacy earlier would seem to me to plant the seed of ideas larger than abstract mathematical logic without doing damage to the logic itself.

Let us look now at the question of co-operation. It is critical to both economic development and the evolution of a society that is capable of internal harmony, that the co-operative spirit should become part of a people's instinct for action. Jamaican social attitudes represent an interesting case study in this regard. On the one hand colonialism and slavery combined to fashion a society which had little natural gift for co-operation. Colonialism is, of necessity, divisive in its impact upon a society except for those moments when the ruled rise up to overthrow their rulers. With that exception, however, colonialism creates an external focus of power and distributes favours not as a reward for contribution to the social group but in the form of a kind of systematised bribery to secure acquiescence in the process of exploitation. Faced with this power nexus, men tend to scramble for favours at each other's expense. If the pattern of power persists for long enough this breeds attitudes which reflect each individual's scramble to survive.

Against this divisive influence must be set, however, the effects of poverty and class exploitation. Jamaican society reflects one area in which the spirit of co-operation is instinctive and provides a key to established patterns of behaviour. The descendants of the slaves who escaped to the hills and retained a sense of solidarity in the face of an otherwise alien society display a

marked aptitude for co-operation. This is reflected in traditional
patterns of behaviour like the swapping of work days. Under
this system the farmers in an area will gather at one field on a
Sunday to help one member of the group till the soil. In due
course the beneficiary of the process does the same for his
neighbours. In much the same way and for largely the same
reasons, the workers who live in urban centres and who share
a long experience of poverty due to wage exploitation have
developed similar patterns. For example, the families that live in
a tenement yard in downtown Kingston develop a system of
communal social welfare called 'share pot'. In this arrangement,
the families whose providers are in jobs at any given moment
literally share their food with their less fortunate neighbours.
This represents a communal response to the harsh reality of
poverty and economic insecurity. Furthermore, the instinct for
co-operation between members of a tenement yard goes deeper
than the response of a group to the pressure of poverty. It is also
reinforced by class overtones which obviously share a common
root with the parallel phenomenon among the rural farmers
whose attitudes involve a declaration of independence from the
slave masters. Hence, it is common to find a group of workers
contributing from their wages at the week-end to support one of
their colleagues who has been suspended as an act of discipline.
There is no question but that the workers who ignore their own
domestic pressures for this act of generosity are both extending
their ghetto experience to the work place and, simultaneously,
declaring their independence from the employer.

It has been fascinating to observe in Jamaica how far this
social impulse has withstood the influence of a highly
sophisticated worker-management relationship as this has
emerged since 1938. There is, after all, a certain irony in a
situation where management and trade union sit down and agree
that suspension without pay is a necessary and desirable deterrent
to certain kinds of action only to find that the members of the
union, and even signatories to a labour management contract,
will contradict the intention of an agreed disciplinary cause in
response to a deeper social impulse.

There are latent in the Jamaican situation, therefore, forces
that tend towards and against the co-operative spirit. The educational process must begin with recognition of this fact and use

it as the starting point for the reinforcement of the positive tendency. At the academic level there should be a strong civics content to education dealing with absolute frankness with both the positive and the negative forces which operate naturally in the society and showing how the negative forces may be overcome and the positive forces made relevant to the future. Equally we should inculcate the deepest pride in the untutored and instinctive patterns of behaviour of the people so that the call for national co-operation is seen as an extension of a magnificent thing that the people created for themselves as their own response to pressure.

Simultaneously, the syllabus should provide for group tasks which need to be tackled together and which call for co-operation for their successful implementation. With a little thought it is not difficult to evolve a whole series of activities beginning at the earliest age which involve children co-operatively.

In many ways the practical steps which can be undertaken at the educational level to develop a spirit of co-operation in children which may last them into later life, overlap very closely the techniques which must be employed to establish attitudes towards work. Insofar as work attitudes are concerned, one distinguishes a general and a particular problem. At the general level it would be true to say that Jamaica has never had a period of its history in which it has accepted the work ethic. This is so because in the condition of slavery, work becomes a form of torture imposed by one group upon another. In the postcolonial period the disproportion of economic power between the former slave masters and the freed slaves was so great as to create little change in the working relationship to accompany the admittedly monumental change in the legal relationship which had taken place. Thus, the great majority of the Jamaican people came to the adventure of freedom with attitudes towards work that reflected the misery of their historical experience. Instead of work being seen as the means by which a man expresses the creativity in himself while he earns his daily bread – or even as a healthy necessity in the pursuit of his daily bread – work is seen as a condition imposed by a master upon a servant as the price of the servant's survival.

In a more particular sense and against the background of the general attitude which has been created historically, we find the intense stigma that attaches to particular kinds of work. Hence, manual labour which was the slave's lot is seen against the backdrop of the memory of slavery. Nor do we dare to dismiss this analysis as fanciful. Anyone who has shared the experience of workers in Jamaican industry will notice that the instinctive response by workers to what they deem to be unreasonable pressure is to condemn that pressure as 'slave driving'. Naturally, therefore, the more unpleasant kinds of work reflect the same historically conditioned tendency to resist.

Obviously, a country cannot develop if there is a neurotic attitude towards work. Rapid development cannot be sustained by negative work attitudes. On the other hand, this is not a problem that will respond to rhetorical injunction. An immaculately attired politician calling for a hard day's work from a field labourer or street cleaner will find himself floundering upon the rock of credibility. To a certain extent such a politician can help by picking up a shovel and setting an example and can contribute to the total educational process in this way. However, enduring solutions must be sought amongst the members of the generation. But even here we will only succeed if we begin with a frank recognition of the problem and bring the resources of educational technique to bear upon it. And it is here that we find the close link between the development of the co-operative spirit and the development of a positive work ethic.

Children love *doing* things. They love doing them with their hands as indeed do many adults during their leisure time. Obviously, the stigma that attaches to manual work is not instinctive but derives in the main from social forces. During childhood then, we have a golden opportunity to instil in people a sense of the naturalness of work and the satisfaction which it can provide; and this can be accomplished while children learn that the experience is heightened when it is shared. Obviously, in an agricultural country children should devote a substantial portion of their school time working together to make things grow. Later, they should become involved in the marketing of their crops, the recording of their expenditures and the measurement of their profit. Equally, in a country which is short of mechanical skills, every primary school should have its model car and model tractor which the older boys strip down and re-assemble; and its dress shop where the girls master the rudiments of the garment industry. All this should be organized in a economic activity with inputs and rewards at a time when the discovery of life is a source of excitement and joy.

Nor does any of this need to inhibit the youngster who is a natural individualist. He or she will remain free to pursue his or her own natural road. In a libertarian society the educational process must retain the flexibility to accommodate individuality while instilling the lessons of group responsibility. Granted the fact of early receptivity, we may be sure that the average child will be profoundly influenced by these positive and creative early influences. The educational system which we brought from colonialism into independence had no positive elements of this sort at all because it was designed for a society which took its attitudes for granted and, hence, saw education as exclusively concerned with skill.

People are unlikely to respond to the positive suggestions or influences of their education if they are unsure of their own identity. And so the system must be constantly concerned with the problem of self-perception. In terms of formal education, some responses are obvious. Our history must have a strong, realistic, national focus and should explore every example of achievement. Every slave uprising should be the subject of exciting adventure tales so that we relate to our own Robin Hoods. Equally importantly, the educational system must come to grips with the question of blackness and the place of Africa. The many people in the Black Caribbean who rationalise their own racial insecurity by dismissing our African heritage as irrelevant do so because they have never faced, in themselves, the scars that have been inflicted by colonial history. They prefer, unconsciously, to hide their own uncertainties behind a mask of shame. Nor can one be without sympathy since we must face the myths of Caucasian superiority from across the chasms of doubt that have been created by the conscious distortions of history which underlay our early education until very recently. However, I am satisfied that the citizen of the Black Caribbean will never be at peace with himself until he makes his peace with Africa. To this day a black Jamaican will respond to the misdeeds of a black acquaintance with withering contempt as coming from a 'nigger who doesn't know better'. An uneasy self-loathing lurks beneath the surface all the time. Obviously, there must be a total response to this problem and all of it cannot be generated from within the society alone since part of the problem is external.

Many of our psychological difficulties stem from our perception of the world around us and in particular our comparative assessment of white and black history. Thus while we grant the primacy of the locally focused solution we dare not ignore the wider context. For every effort that is made to instil national self-confidence there must be a parallel effort to set our African, and hence our black heritage in a legitimate context. To this day if you were to ask the average Jamaican to say what he thought were the accomplishments of Black Africa he would probably be aware of Nkrumah and Kenyatta as national liberators. He would certainly be conscious of His Imperial Majesty Haile Selassie as a spiritual symbol. After that he might be hard put to it to go beyond Kipchoge Keino of distance-running fame. There certainly would be no awareness whatsoever of the great artistic achievements of most African tribes nor of the gift for inner social harmony which is a distinctive African achievement in marked contrast to Europe's increasingly catastrophic failure at this level. To deal with all this it is necessary that our educational system should include a strong stream of African studies so that the historical imbalances which centre around the European myth can be redressed by the truth. Equally, there should be the most vigorous promotion of cultural exchange so that African dance, drama, painting and sculpture along with its Caribbean counterparts should be constantly on display in both regions. Only by means such as these can our own experience be enriched by exposure to a new and relevant stream of creativity and our reaction to our own blackness take on an increasingly natural character.

Art is the mirror through which a society perceives itself; and it is a mirror that must be held up to young societies constantly if they are to achieve a sense of their separate identity in the world. Clearly, therefore, the development of the latent artistic talent of a society is important to its growth and critical to the process of psychological transformation with which we are concerned.

Jamaica's dynamic artistic movement is part of the process by which we first attained and later experienced independence. But this has tended to be a small, though intense, part of the total social experience. Artists have sprung from all sections of Jamaican society but the audience has tended to be predominantly amongst the intellectual middle class. If the whole society is to develop in an egalitarian way art must reflect the total social experience and be appreciated by the society as a whole. Often the failure of the artist to communicate with large areas of the society is a consequence of lack of training coupled with a failure to make art available to all kinds of audiences in all geographical locations. In other words, the educational process must first recognise art, in this widest sense of painting, sculpture, poetry, drama, literature, the theatre, music, dancing and the rest, as an indispensable element in the process of transformation. Thereafter exposure to art must be planned.

The young must be made aware of art so that they may acquire the taste for it. The logistical problems of making art available in all the geographical regions of a country have got to be mastered and can only be effectively handled by government action. We cannot afford to ignore these things because of the part that art must play in national development. For example, plays that reflect the tensions or the aspirations of the society cannot be seen only where audiences can afford to pay the 'economic' price to see them. They must be made available to everyone because they are part of the means by which the society may come to understand its own problems by seeing them articulated with clarity and passion. It is our responsibility as a nation not 'to bring to the people' but to bring art and the people together.

In this connection it is interesting to observe that Jamaica, which shares with all other countries of the world, a strong heritage of folk art has done a lot to preserve this hertitage. In fact folk art is an established part of the Jamaican entertainment complex. However, there has sprung up in recent years a new form of folk art in the field of popular music. These are the singers who bespeak the tragedy and the pain, the hopes and the aspirations of the ghetto. In their music, the reggae, there is eloquently foreshadowed the concept of a just society as they protest its absence. These artists are largely untrained. At the same time we commit resources to institutions that train young musicians in the disciplines of western classical music. Here is a marriage which must be made and consummated in the interest of transformation and development. Reggae artists should be brought into the stream of musical education which would be of considerable advantage to their techniques. Simultaneously, they would enrich our music and perhaps help to give us our first major contribution to the serious music of the world. Here we might have an art form that was rooted in a commitment to justice as it bespoke an idealistic vision of what we might accomplish.

Alongside these conscious adjustments in the focus of formal education must be set a number of parallel activities. For example, I suggest that a developing society cannot afford to leave the function of advertising to be determined solely by the private sector without reference to national objectives. Modern advertising has a powerful influence upon attitudes and when its techniques are directed solely to the promotion of a product, its social consequences can be considerable. Take, for example, the problem of work ethic. Advertising which is based on the 'give away' is actually working counter to the national interest and can help to undo every gain which one seeks to achieve through education and public leadership. Equally, the constant repetition of the theme of white beauty involves the danger that black self-confidence will continue to be undermined. Black must be beautiful in a black country and advertising can help product and nation alike if it says so.

Equally, there is the question of sport. There are purists who contend that competitive sport is a bad thing because it appeals to the aggressive instinct. The truth is that aggressiveness is a part of the human personality in modern society and will not be contained by being ignored. The secret of successful social engineering lies in creating channels through which human personality can express itself and in designing those channels so that they are consistent with the larger national objectives of development within a framework of order. Organized sport is, therefore, singularly capable of teaching this lesson without ever having to preach. It is not for nothing that the English can attribute their success at Waterloo to the playing fields of Eton. And the point is not that the playing fields of Eton made men warlike so much as that it made them capable of discipline under pressure. In any event, one has only to look at the behaviour patterns of young people in situations of urban poverty. Left to itself young, unguided spills on to the streets because home is not a place to stay and there is no sports field on which they can express their instinct for aggressive group activity. Gang crime is the result and in today's world it is all too often lent the romantic sanction of heroic example by the violent films which glorify criminal leadership of one sort or another. Sports heroes can supply the answer to the romantic needs of the young just as completely as any other and with far more healthy results. I am convinced that organized sport is a critical tool in any strategy of national development.

Finally, we must consider the problem of adult literacy. Many developing societies have concluded that the adult illiterate must be treated as expendable on the grounds that resources are scarce and that other needs must be met. I reject this thesis. I share the view which has been held by other leaders of developing nations such as Castro and Nyerere, that it is impossible to create either a modern economy or a just society if a substantial proportion of the adult population is denied the social tools, reading and writing, which are indispensable to full participation in either the economic or social systems of a modern nation state. The implications are both practical and psychological. On the one hand, it is a contradiction in terms to speak of economic development and a solution to problems like unemployment in the absence of the most fundamental of all human skills. Furthermore, reading and writing is increasingly a pre-requisite for economic participation as modern economies grow more and more sophisticated.

At the psychological level the individual cannot feel himself a full citizen if he is excluded from so important a part of the common experience. Hence, any society that has set itself the objective of social justice based upon equality cannot tolerate substantial illiteracy. Nor can it hope to accomplish economic transformation. Quite apart, however, from the reasons that make action imperative there is the question of the effect of the action itself. Early Jamaican experience of its national literacy drive which was launched as a total assault in 1972, indicates that the bringing together of large numbers of volunteers to teach literacy with those who seek to learn, enriches the experience of both and creates a bond between the two groups of immeasurable social value. It is as if a bridge of common action were being built across the chasm of class. At an even deeper level, it is my belief that the successful accomplishment of a national task in which moral overtones concerning society and justice predominate, can be a critical experience for the nation itself. To succeed in the task of eliminating illiteracy in a short space of time, means that a society has been able to define a goal for itself, to share a common confidence that that goal is moral and to demonstrate the capacity to attain it through collective action. By that act a nation can proclaim its capacity for the just ordering of its affairs and for the transformation of an aspect of its life. This common experience can, thus, establish a psychological foundation for national self-confidence while laying the practical foundations for material accomplishment.

No examination of society and education would be complete without considering the problem of class. Post-colonial Caribbean society is completely class dominated and Jamaica is, perhaps, the member of the Black Caribbean community in which class boundaries are most deeply entrenched. Indeed, there is a school of social anthropology that has actually contended that class divisions in Jamaica are so deeply rooted as to create the conditions of a plural society. I myself doubt if this is totally valid but there is sufficient evidence to support a plausible argument.

Class divisions and social justice are incompatible. Hence, if the latter is to be achieved the former must yield. However, as with all human behaviour patterns, class attitudes are deeply entrenched. The difficulty of the task leads many political leaders of idealistic commitment to shrink from the remedies that are required because these are drastic. It is clear that the process of transformation from a stratified to a classless society must begin with the educational process. Later, positive change can be sustained by forms of political and economic organization and particularly as these create access to the decision-making process at all levels. But none of this will succeed in the future if the process does not begin with the fundamentals. The educational system must be set the conscious task of overcoming home influences since the latter will tend to perpetuate existing pre-ᴊudices. In a sense, the educational system must create new generations who evolve their own social orders as an extension of new concepts which they discover together in their formative years. Happily, this is a moment of great historical opportunity because of the almost universal disenchantment that the young feel towards the values, habits and attitudes of their elders.

I have already indicated a number of areas to do with the spirit of co-operation and attitudes to work which can help to create the climate of a classless society. These must be supported by clear and positive teaching in the civics stream of the educational system about the equality of man and his place in a society which is intended to reflect that ideal. But when one remembers the total implications of a classless society, which are nothing less than a social system in which upward and downward mobility are determined exclusively by individual merit subject only to the right of all to a minimum share, one realises that nothing less than total measures will accomplish this. I suggest that two pre-conditions must be met. First of all the educational system must begin with a single stream of basic and primary education in which the quality of the facilities that are available are the same for all children. Society must make these facilities the best that resources can provide. Within these facilities, there must be room to accommodate the special needs of the handicapped and the backward. Equally, provision must be made to deal with the claims of the gifted and the talented. It is impossible to reconcile the notion of a society of equality with unequal educational facilities. The moment any class or group can buy themselves a better start in education for their offspring they have laid the foundations of a class system by conferring advantage upon a child through efforts other than its own. There can be no compromise about this if one is serious about egalitarianism.

The second pre-condition is to be found in the notion of non-military, universal national service. Even if our educational system begins with equal facilities, the natural talent of some children will gain them proper educational advantages later on. The more gifted children will end up in university and so on into the higher reaches of the economy; those of medium talent will do well in the secondary system and the others may never get beyond a trade. As this process of separation by talent and aptitude takes place, there is, once again, the danger of sowing the seeds of elitism which can in due course stratify itself into a new class system. It is crucial, therefore, that even the most brilliant student who wins for himself the most exceptional place in the educational system should be required to give back to its society a period of free service. This period should be spent working with and beside young people of all levels of talents and varieties of background. Quite apart from the contribution that this makes to the mobilising of skills for national purposes, it has a deeper value by reinforcing egalitarianism by action. More than this, it can help to keep alive in a young mind the notion that one owes one's place in society to society itself and that some part of the commitment of oneself as a human being must be to the social grouping as a whole. To the extent that the just society is committed to equality and rests upon service, a period of compulsory, non-military, national service which brings all people together in the service of their nation before they move finally into the adult world will reinforce both commitments in the young mind.

F

5

Change and the Basic Institutions

Let us assume that we have distinguished the elements of social justice, defined equality and identified a possible strategy for their attainment. Let us assume, further, that there is a government with the will to attempt the transformation that is necessary. In the context of a free society a substantial problem will remain to be overcome before one can hope to translate intention into accomplishment. The problem arises from the severe limitations upon action that are imposed on a government by the institutions of a free society. Therefore, any strategy must be centrally concerned with the institutions themselves, their traditional attitudes and objectives and must seek answers to the question: How can these institutions be made a part of the general effort at social reconstruction? This is critical to the entire exercise because the major institutions of a democracy can virtually paralyse a government's attempts to create change. On the other hand, these same institutions, if they were to work in concert with a government, could not only accelerate the pace of change but help to mobilise people to enthusiastic participation in the processes of change and even help to fashion the shape of change. This is an area, therefore, that requires careful analysis.

It is first of all important to identify the institutions themselves and to examine the traditional role of these institutions in terms of past attitudes and objectives. We must then consider the critical question: How can one hope to persuade free institutions to the acceptance of new objectives? And finally, we must look at the new role which institutions can and must play if new objectives are to be achieved.

In the Jamaican situation one can identify nine institutions with which one must deal. To these should be added three special groups which must be considered separately for special reasons. The institutions are: the political parties, the trade unions, the Church, the teachers, the commodity and the producers associations (such as the National Farmers Union, the Jamaica Manufacturers Association, the Chamber of Commerce and the like), the voluntary associations (such as service clubs and building societies), the professions, the Civil Service and the machinery of government, and the Press. The three special groups are women, the minorities and youth.

The traditional institutions of a free society have been concerned, in the main, with the pursuit of sectional interest. Nor is this surprising. The interpretation placed upon freedom in these societies has not only permitted, but positively invited, action which reflects the presumed legitimacy of self-interest. Hence, institutions organized around identifiable sectors of society have been primarily concerned with their own interests and have only secondarily considered these in the context of the wider interests of society. A classic example of this attitude was provided by a former head of the General Motors Corporation, who, upon being appointed Secretary for Defence by the late President Eisenhower remarked that 'what was good for General Motors was good for the United States'. Only rarely have institutions begun by accepting the view that the national interest must provide the framework within which to pursue sectional interests. Hence, although politics is concerned with the ordering of national affairs, political parties constantly take incredible and knowing risks with the national good in the pursuit of power. It has been customary for most trade unions in a free society to repudiate any suggestion that the pursuit of their members' interest may be modified or contained as a consequence of an understanding of national requirements. So too with businessmen who traditionally expect the freedom to maximize profits without regard to the needs of their customers or of the country at large.

A second problem which arises when one looks at the question of a change in basic institutional attitudes flows from a repudiation of an alternative course traditionally associated with totalitarianism. If free societies have been associated with sectional licence, closed societies have reflected state regimentation. In the one case there has been no attempt to invite national consensus through dialogue. In the other case national consensus is ordered without dialogue and dissent is stifled. An important consequence of the observation of totalitarian methods has been to cloud the question of consensus in a free society. National consensus becomes confused with totalitarian method instead of being understood as necessary to the functioning of society itself and a result that can be secured through dialogue. This has had the unfortunate effect of providing an excuse for sectional leadership to resist any form of dialogue which might lead to national consensus on the ground that consensus itself is a totalitarian phenomenon.

Finally, colonialism made it inevitable that institutional activity should act upon the presumption that authority is alien. If authority is felt to be alien then the pusuit of narrow, sectional interest will appear, by contrast, to be moral. As a consequence, colonialism provided a climate in which the dichotomy between local institutions and state power was total. The fact that some institutions were subservient to the colonial authority in no way modifies the argument. In that context subservience reflected a recognition of reality and was the price that was paid for protection. It did not imply a recognition that authority was the larger framework within which sectional interest was pursued. Since the power was foreign it could not be identified with the totality of local interests and hence no philosophical ground for respect could exist.

Against this background one must ask the question: How, within the assumptions and the accepted methodology of a free society, can one hope to persuade institutions to accept a larger set of objectives to which the pursuit of their sectional interest must be subject? Obviously, this is a process of considerable difficulty because it involves, in the first place, the reversal of a historical tendency; and in the second, may be thought by many to run counter to the very nature of a free society. Part of the answer, of course, lies in a massive and persistent process of political education. Once people can be brought to understand that freedom must be pursued in the context of the good of society because it is only a stable society that can create the conditions within which there is any freedom to be enjoyed, it becomes possible to embark upon a dialogue about objectives. In post-colonial, developing societies like Jamaica the first task is to make people aware of the fundamental change in the relationship between the individual, the sectional group and the society at large, on the one hand, and political power on the other, which

CHANGE AND BASIC INSTITUTIONS

has in fact taken place. It is vital to establish the fact of this change and to ensure that it is understood by every citizen. In short, people must be led to understand that both survival and progress are now their own responsibility. Once this is established, the next task is to involve people, through the politics of participation, in a constantly unfolding dialogue about objectives and methods which not only establishes the primacy of a moral social purpose, but, through participation, creates a climate in which people and institutions begin to feel that they share in the authorship of the concepts to which they are asked to dedicate themselves.

Naturally, the sanction of the law will always have to be used to deal with persons or groups who will not accept larger national purposes. But there is nothing new in this. The law already regulates our relationship to each other and to society in a thousand ways. In part, what we are concerned with here is an extension of those areas to include relationships as they are affected by the larger social purposes that we have defined. But the process cannot stop with the law nor must it depend upon the law exclusively. Much that we must seek to accomplish will only happen through the free and enthusiastic participation of people. You can pass a law which makes it compulsory for every child to go to a school that is part of a single, egalitarian system. You cannot pass a law that makes a teacher teach enthusiastically or a group of workers put their best into the job. The law can restrict and contain but it cannot mobilise and enthuse. Hence, even in the matter of seeking the transformation of institutional attitudes, one's purpose must be to engage voluntary enthusiasm. Nor is this so only in response to the philosophical concepts of freedom. The notion rests finally upon the belief that men will contribute to society most effectively where they do so on the basis of a free choice and where the choice of right comes in response to understanding rather than compulsion.

Our fourth consideration which was the part which institutions can play, is best dealt with as we consider each institution in turn.

THE POLITICAL PARTY

The first and perhaps most critical of the institutions with which we are concerned is the political party itself. Surprising as it may seem, the political party is not only the most important single agent working either for or against change but is often the institution most likely to oppose change. This tends to be so for three main reasons. First of all, one must remember that a political party is a collection of people drawn from various walks of life in a society. As such, the collective result, which is the party itself, tends to reflect the prejudices, the traditional habits of thought and all the fears and foibles that are characteristic of the population at large. To the extent, therefore that a post-colonial society has been historically conditioned so too will we find that the members of the political party will themselves be the prisoners of that experience and will tend to carry the prejudices of that experience over into the modes of thought of the organization. Nor is this as surprising as it may seem on the surface. One might be tempted to argue that the experience of fighting for freedom would lead to a process of intellectual disassociation from all things colonial. This view ignores, however, the subconscious influence of the colonial experience itself. It is one thing to demand freedom and to fight the colonial master for it. It is another thing to rid the mind of the subtle influences that have permeated the mind, through the workings of colonialism, from birth. Hence, it is not unusual to see a party passionately committed to nationalism behaving like a colonial institution once freedom is attained.

Then again, one must understand the relationship between political parties and currents of popular opinion. In a democratic situation the political party is, of necessity, dependent upon general popular opinion and, hence, sensitive to it. It is in this context that one has to examine the effect of change upon a society.

A man's instinctive reaction to change is to fear it. This reflects the primeval response to the unknown and is as old as man himself. Nor can one hope to deal with change in a purely rational way because the fear, though rooted in a deep common sense, is not necessarily in itself a rational response to an objective situation. People who are experiencing genuine and chronic distress will often react violently to a proposal for change merely because they do not understand it and are by no means convinced that any change would be for the better. Such is the nature of man's attachment to life, which he often undertands in terms of the familiar that men will often seem to prefer the deepest poverty to the unknown. In this context one must understand that terms like 'familiar' and 'unknown' do not only relate to external, concrete things. They also embrace traditional habits of thought and assumptions about society and its relationships.

The politics of change, as it relates to the creation of a just society, involves both material and attitudinal areas of action leading to transformation. Thus it must involve a constant assault upon the familiar, at both conscious and unconscious levels. It is inevitable that a continuing thrust for change will tend to breed a continuing reaction of fear since change cannot be restricted merely to the building of more and better roads but involves much else if a just society is to be accomplished. Indeed the process requires the acceptance of many changes that are not necessarily popular but may represent the price that has to be paid for more houses and better roads. There is a sense, therefore, in which all significant political change involves constant ferment. This means that the political party which is acting as the principal agent of change is subject to constant pressure as change produces fear and fear produces a clamour for the process to stop. Political parties are by their nature sensitive to public opinion and since the latter is disturbed by change, the natural response of a political party may be to put pressure upon its leadership and the government which has been drawn from its ranks to slow down if not to stop. Situations in which the rank and file of a political party clamour for change when they are in opposition but tend to panic if a government of their creation genuinely pursues change when in power are a common sight.

To all this must be added a third consideration. It is in the nature of political parties to be concerned with the acquisition and keeping of power and the distribution of favours. In the democratic context the political parties live with the constant reality of competition. They have to be concerned with maintaining election machines which can man polling stations with transporting voters and influencing people to vote in a certain way. Simultaneously, they tend to be under constant pressure to distribute favours not only to members of the organization, but to supporters in the widest sense. In the Jamaican political system which is based on geographical constituencies and is in other respects a fair approximation of the Westminster model, the Member of Parliament and, consequently, the constituency organization becomes inextricably involved in things like provision of jobs, the distribution of houses, pressure for water supplies, street lights and sidewalks; and indeed all the basic elements of the pattern of 'felt needs'. As a result, a political party can become so involved in the minutiae of political organization and constituency requirements as to lose touch with its avowed national objectives. This can make it extremely vulnerable to the currents of fear that are generated by fundamental change. Unable to handle popular panic, the party membership often takes refuge in the paraphernalia of its own patterns of familiarity. It is quite common, therefore, to hear the middle rank leadership of a political party which is attempting fundamental change exclaim in anguish that all they want their government to do is provide a few more jobs and a few more houses. Although this may be an accurate reflection of 'felt need' at that moment in time it may completely ignore the other changes which are the pre-condition of the ability to provide the jobs and the houses. At this stage one is hearing the *cri de coeur* of an organization which is not geared intellectually or emotionally to handle the popular fear.

Therefore, one must begin by recognizing that political parties are not committed to change by the rhetoric of political philosophy. The members of a party may applaud the rhetoric and warm to the philosophy when both may be enjoyed from the safety of a pavilion high above the arena of action. When, however, the rhetoric and the philosophy come to be tested in the field they take on a different aspect and the party members' instinct is to run for cover declaring that they still believe in the philosophy but think it might well be shelved for another day and a more propitious occasion. However, there will never be a more 'propitious occasion' for the politics of change; hence the advantages that seem to attach to 'another day' are illusory. Change will always occasion fear and fear untended can escalate with disconcerting speed into panic. A political party which is involved in a philosophical intention to re-fashion society in terms of idealistic alternatives, must understand the problems it will face as the agent of change. Consequently, it must be con-

sciously organized to be capable of tackling the politics of change
and the problems which beset it.

One cannot by any means ignore the organizational functions
which are concerned with elections and votes nor the service
functions which deal with 'felt needs'. What is necessary, however, is to create as tough and as highly organized a cadre of
leadership devoted to the understanding of change and its problems as are the cadres which deal with organization and the
servicing of constituency needs. Furthermore, a party of change
must begin by understanding that its first responsibility and
first tasks lie in the field of political education to which all else,
however important, is secondary. The process of political education must begin as an internal function. This means that the
political party must be committed to a clear, unequivocal,
philosophical view of society about which there can be no compromise. It must also possess a sure means by which the translation of its philosophy into programmes of action is accomplished.
Preferably this should involve considerable participation in terms
of dialogue between those who are charged with the final formulation of policy, on the one hand, and the rank and file of the
political organization on the other. This dialogue should be an
ongoing process organized at the group, constituency and
national levels so as to provide a constant flow of inward and out-
ward information, opinion and argument, as the outer reaches of
the organization feed in popular reactions to the planners and
policy makers at the centre and as the latter feed out the programmes of action to the members of the organization. Then
again, the organization must understand its role in relation to the
people at large. The objective must be to engage, within the scope
of the organization, the widest possible range of people and to
provide the political leadership which is capable of creating and
maintaining a ferment of political education throughout an ever
growing organization. Once this has been achieved the purpose
of the organization is to establish the first principles of the party's
political philosophy, to explain the programmes of action which
are necessary if the philosophy is to be translated into action and
to enlist popular help by inviting constructive criticism. In part,
the exercise is aimed at the mobilization of understanding; and in
part, it is aimed at the establishment of a participatory relationship in which, through the workings of the political party, the

people at large are made to feel a sense of responsibility for the various national programmes and popular efforts that are necessary to the process of transformation.

In this sense, the politics of change demand the creation of a mass political organization which is capable of organizing mass response, mass understanding and mass involvement in the processes of change.

A special aspect of the role of a political party which needs consideration is the relationship which should exist between the party, as an entity, and the government. In the Westminster model, the cabinet is the executive arm of Parliament. However, cabinets have become increasingly exclusive institutions, more and more subject to a 'closed' working method. As a result, the cabinet as an institution, tends to suffer from an increasing isolation from the general membership of Parliament, on the one hand, and the political party on the other. Historically, this has arisen to a certain extent because of the importance of maintaining the principle of collective responsibility within a cabinet. In addition, as modern government has grown ever more complex, the importance of surrounding aspects of government planning with secrecy, has increased. However, a developing country, the government of which depends upon the political party as an instrument of popular communication and mobilization, makes a grave error if it bases its methods of operation on an uncritical transplantation of the Westminister model. Considerable adaptation is necessary and must include devices that ensure that the political party has the capacity to influence the formulation of government policy. Of course one must continue to observe the rules of secrecy and collective responsibility where necessary. However, it is all too easy to create a sense of separation between a government and the political organization upon which it rests by repeatedly formulating policies within the confines of the cabinet room from whence they are announced, often to take an unsuspecting corpus of political leadership by surprise. This quickly leads to alienation of the party from the government which, in turn, can lead to defiant posturings by a government claiming that it is elected to 'rule' and, in aid of its contention, quoting the Westminster precedent.

Clearly, the closest collaboration must exist between the executive of the political party, the general parliamentary group, the workers' movement and the cabinet itself. This can be time-consuming but the investment is indispensable if effective communication and dialogue are to be maintained. What is more, the communication is by no means of value in one direction only. Government itself is given focus and relevance and a quality of 'contact' with the people and their 'felt needs', if it maintains a close and continuing dialogue with the political organization. Once again, this illustrates the extent to which the politics of participation, in this case the participation of the political party in the governmental decision-making process, depends upon the willingness to take pains coupled with great institutional flexibility and ingenuity. Where the will and ingenuity are present, however, the effort is justified by the degree of popular mobilization that can be achieved.

What about the other parties? Suppose they are not committed to change? Suppose they organize a constant flow of propaganda designed to exploit the fears of the people? These are questions that are frequently asked. At another level, it is contended that the political dialogue which is fundamental to the democratic process is essentially conservative in effect and tends, always, to put a brake upon the processes of change.

To the first contention one is tempted to reply: So what! If another party, or other parties work against change it is surely up to the party of change to out-organize, out-argue, out-teach, out-explain and out-perform them. If one accepts that challenge the resultant focusing of energy is good for the party and the maintenance of dialogue good for the country in the long run. As to the second contention, it is true as far as it goes. But the argument ignores a parallel truth. Although it is fair to say that the democratic process tends to put a brake upon change, it is also fair to say that it creates a pressure for change. Historically, the forces of conservatism have undergone at least as much progressive transformation as have the forces of change been subject to restraint. The process of the dialectic has constantly modified both forces and society itself represents a new synthesis at any moment of time. The real challenge is to the forces of change which must constantly modify and adapt their strategies and techniques as they seek to sweep society along new paths leading to the ultimate goal.

THE TRADE UNION MOVEMENT

Among the more remarkable but paradoxical institutions of modern democracy is the trade union movement. Ironic as this may seem, it is certainly the institution which fits least readily into a strategy of change. The union movement was born at a time when the worker throughout the world was regarded as a kind of sub-species of mankind distinguishable from the machine he tended, by little save his ability to talk. The worker's problem consisted not only in the fact that his wages could scarcely support his family, but more importantly in the fact that the rest of society assumed that this was his natural lot. Thus, when the union movement came into being to commence the long struggle for decent wages and working conditions, it had to fight far more than the natural tendency of the employer to hold on to the lion's share of the wealth which was created by economic activity. The union movement had also to fight a power structure which was completely dominated and controlled by the employer; and the belief, on the part of the rest of society, that the worker's struggle for a living wage was contrary to a natural order and therefore a threat to society itself.

Thus, from the outset the union movement had to fight on three fronts: it had to fight against the immediate employer; it had to fight the power apparatus of the state; and it had to fight the established assumptions of public opinion. More than is the case with most institutions, the movement survived by closing its ranks to form a tight, sectional phalanx. To fight the employer called for a capacity to make extreme sacrifices, involving long periods of hunger during strikes, the ability to resist the temptations with which shrewd employers sought to divide the movement, and even the willingness to face death or injury on the picket line. To fight the state apparatus required a capacity to summon raw determination and that moral force which exacts total obedience because it rests on faith. After all, upon what else could the worker depend. To fight established public opinion demanded the assertion by the movement of the primacy and ultimate legitimacy of its own cause. All this was true of the union movement of Britain throughout the second half of the nineteenth century and right up to the advent of the Second World War. It was true of the American union movement throughout the first half of the twentieth century. It was true in Jamaica from the birth of the modern trade union movement in 1938 and for at least the first twenty years of its existence.

However inevitable this process may have been, it has left its scars and created a movement which does not easily respond to appeals made in the national interest. Its historical experience has left its thinking profoundly rooted in the principle that survival depends upon the capacity to fight the rest of the nation. Consequently, we find all too often that the union movement has elevated a past requirement of survival into a permanent law of behaviour sanctioned by the assertion of a high moral purpose. Hence, the problem of persuading the trade union movement to relate its own actions to some national concept and plan involves more than ordinary difficulty. With most institutions the problem consists mainly of dealing with the natural selfishness of mankind raised to the higher degree of group interest. This co-exists with a frank admission that the group interest may run counter to the national interest. In the case of the union movement, however, we are dealing with an institution that was compelled by history and circumstance to assume that the 'national interest' was an alien concept invoked by selfish groups to oppress the worker. Everything in the unionist's conditioning, therefore, tends to make him deeply suspicious of national appeals and with good historical cause.

If we take Jamaica'a case we can readily see some of the difficulties which arise, as a consequence of union action, for rational, national planning. For example, wages in the so-called premium industries such as bauxite, petroleum and cement, run between four and six times as high as wages in the agricultural sector for identical jobs. This is a consequence of a supposedly free economy in which neither profits nor prices have reflected any consideration of the national interest and where, as a consequence, wage fixing has been an arbitrary exercise reflecting entirely fortuitous factors such as levels of profitability, the relative bargaining power of employers and workers and sheer accidents of leadership, character, personality and ability on either or both sides of the bargaining table. Clearly, however, vastly differing wages for identical work are inconsistent with notions of equality. Further, large wage differentials of an arbitrary nature can make the rational disposition of manpower resources extremely difficult. Equally, to draw upon experience of a more general character, one can see how difficult it can become to ask for a policy of wage restraint even where this is accompanied by strong action in relation to prices and profits. To the union movement such an appeal, in whatever context of parallel and similar action, appears as a familiar invasion of right rather than a simple extension of national planning.

How then, can we hope to create a situation in which the union movement becomes involved in and responsive to national planning seen in terms of an overall concept of the national interest? The answer, I suggest, must be explored at two levels. First, we must consider the question of how to involve the union movement in national planning. Second, the union movement must begin to evolve a new perception of its role in society. As it happens, both these developments are dependent upon the acceptance of a new concept of the worker's role in the society and of his place in the economy as expressed by the relationship between the worker and the ownership of resources on the one hand, and the decision-making process, on the other. If our egalitarian convictions and our concern for social justice lead us to the understanding that workers should share in both the ownership of resources and the processes which decide upon their use, then the view which we take of the relationship between the union movement and the processes of government takes on a new aspect. Equally, the obligation of the union movement to its membership is automatically redefined. Assuming that it is our intention to evolve this new status for the worker, let us consider the union in society and the union and its membership in turn.

A society in general and its government in particular have a responsibility to seek to involve the trade union movement in every conceivable aspect of public life. The union movement should be invited to participate in national planning bodies, statutory organizations, in local government deliberations and at every level at which the society takes decisions. Furthermore, this should be no mere public relations exercise but should seek meaningful involvement of the movement in the decision-making process. For its part, the union movement should seek this kind of involvement and welcome the invitation to participate. More and more the union movement needs to recognise that its duty to its membership cannot stop at the factory gate but must explore every aspect of the worker's life. This implies the positive acceptance of a responsibility on the part of the union movement to seek to influence every activity which has any bearing, however remote, on the life of workers and their families. It also implies a re-thinking of fundamental objectives. Near the surface of every unionist's thinking lurks the notion that conflict between the movement and society is part of a natural order. The unionist must now re-think his basic postulates beginning with the notion that a well-ordered and just society would make that conflict unnecessary. Of course, this is a hard pill for the professional unionist to swallow. Since he conceives of his role in combative terms he is all too ready to suspect that he would have no place in a world that had no conflict. Many unionists, as a consequence, secretly suspect that to accept the creation of a just and conflict-free world as the primary objective of the union movement would be to involve themselves in a self-liquidating exercise. But this is not necessarily so. Once this is grasped it becomes possible to assess a new focus for union activity resting upon the acceptance of the larger objective of social justice. It is with this in mind that we must consider the new functions which the union movement must seek to perform.

The first, and most fundamental of the tasks to which the union movement should set its hand is the development of a strategy designed to move workers increasingly into a position of ownership in the enterprises where they are engaged. This is an enormously difficult and challenging exercise because it involves for societies like Jamaica, completely new initiatives that will have to cut across traditional assumptions. For example, most Jamaican employers begin with the customary assumption that only the payment of cash can lead to the ownership of a share in a business. Work should be accepted as an alternative means of purchasing shares and the society must begin to explore formulae for assessing work, in terms of length of service, and in relation to pre-determined values of share holding. It is possible to work out methods for the acquisition of shares that reflect a blend of service and cash payments which can be made through pay-roll deduction schemes. Obviously, the variations that can be explored are considerable. But the first task is to persuade the unionist that all this is worthwhile since it is quite common to find resistance to the idea.

Opposition stems, presumably, from the fear that shares in the ownership of a business would mitigate the worker's drive for wage increases and so reduce his dependence on his union negotiator. The fear, however, is seen to be unreal as soon as the new challenges are understood. A worker who is part owner of a business is faced with a whole new range of decisions which he must be assisted to make. He must still determine, in his own mind, the question of the wage which he wishes to take home on a regular basis by comparison with the earnings that might accrue to him annually through dividends. In addition he must now become involved in deciding between present earnings, of either sort, and future additional earnings which can accrue to him if he accepts a programme involving the re-investment of profit. All this will enlarge the role of the professional unionist, not eliminate it. It is interesting to observe, for example, that the increasing spread of share ownership in modern Western economies has been accompanied by the rapid development of industries which service shareholders of which the most obvious example is the stock-broking firm. Hence, our problem in terms of trade union attitudes stems from the unionist's own conservatism and irrational fear of change not from any real threat to the union movement itself. This conclusion holds true across the whole spectrum of change which faces the modern trade union.

In addition to the development of a strategy for worker-ownership of industry, is the question of worker involvement in the decision-making process. The ownership of industry leads inevitably to involvement in decisions concerning the development of the industry. The owner is affected by decisions about the distribution of profits, the exploration of new markets, the allocation of resources to research and so on. Hence, ownership invites participation in the decision-making process. In the case of the worker, this process should not stop with the major concerns such as resource allocation. At a more immediate level there is a whole new area of worker participation in management which waits to be explored. Consultation about shop floor decisions, methods of improving productivity, working rules and safety procedures all demand a joint approach if enduring success is to be assured. The success of the business and the creative engagement of the worker are happily inter-dependent in areas such as these. But once again it is going to call for considerable ingenuity to devise the institutions through which all this can be made to happen. To ingenuity must be added the will to explore the possibilities of a new relationship between worker and management. Crucial to this new relationship is the determination to replace conflict with co-operation; and to substitute for the antagonisms inherent in the master-servant relationship that sense of a mutual adventure which is the natural condition of men whose functions may be different but who share a common stake in an enterprise.

Even in the more conventional areas of bargaining, there is the need for increasing attention to ancillary benefits, the acquisition of which serve a national as well as an individual purpose. For example, a vacation leave policy has an essentially private purpose. It may contribute marginally to the success of the vacation industry, but basically it is designed to meet the individual's need for rest without economic dislocation. On the other hand, a savings scheme funded by employer and worker jointly and devoted to the funding of housing schemes goes far beyond the satisfaction of private needs. This exercise embraces a broad national purpose which would be valid in a metropolitan country but reflects an urgent social priority in a developing one. Simultaneously, the diversion of some proportion of possible wage benefits from immediate increases to savings may be intimately related to national effects to fight inflation and may simultaneously contribute to a strategy for encouraging savings.

All this calls for a massive process of education. To begin with there is the need for the re-education of union leadership itself beginning with a new perception of fundamental relationships. This must lead, in turn, to mass education of union membership. If this challenge is met the union movement can become an agent for change, second only to the political party and in so doing can renew its early idealistic promise. The men who challenged the cruel assumptions of the nineteenth century and took the weapons of will and moral purpose to shatter an oppressive establishment, were the agents of a change that was profound in its time. But implicit in this change was no mere amelioration of circumstance. The worker's right to protest stands upon one philosophical foundation: the assumption of his inherent equality. By extension, the same equality cannot mean only the right to protest and to have that protest measured in a wage increase. It is not the wage increase that is fundamental but the equality. A wage increase can lead to an amelioration of personal circumstance but not to a re-ordering of fundamental relationships. It is to the re-ordering of these relationships that today's union movement must address itself if it is to remain true to the ultimate purposes which are implied by the early struggles of the movement.

THE CHURCH

In considering the part that the Church can play in the development of a country like Jamaica, we need to recall that Jamaicans are a church-going people brought up in a strong 'God fearing' tradition. There is deep, instinctive respect for the clergyman. However, this respect has been traditionally associated with guidance in things spiritual, very often by default of temporal concern on the part of the clergyman. On the other hand, there have been denominations, and notably the Baptists, with a strong activist tradition. The Baptist Church played a tremendous part in the development of the early land settlement schemes which followed the abolition of slavery and was constantly in the forefront in the battle for land reform. The national hero Paul Bogle, a Baptist deacon, was hanged by the British for his leadership of the abortive revolution of 1865; his cause was land reform. Sharp and George William Gordon were both Baptist deacons like Bogle and they shared his fate. Gordon is also a national hero.

We now need to analyze two situations. First, one must consider the relationship between Church and State; and, secondly, one must consider the possible role of the Church in relation to the problems which arise in a two or multi-party democracy in the area of communal and national co-operation. In the centuries that have followed St Thomas Aquinas' proclamation of the concept of the separation of Church and State which he described, with simple eloquence as 'twin swords', the Church has been uneasy morally and philosophically about its role in things temporal. Some religious thinkers and, indeed, denominations, have declared that the Church has no temporal concerns whatsoever and must deal exclusively with man's immortal soul and its safe passage to heaven. At the other end of the scale, there have been examples of the Church virtually dominating the temporal life of a country and seeming to accord the most perfunctory attention to the things of the spirit. All Churches, however, have been firmly united in the view that the State must never interfere with, or dictate to, the men of God and often have proved willing to concede a reciprocal separation. In Jamaica, until quite recently, there was a growing mood among all churchmen in this last direction. Since independence, however, this tendency has been substantially reversed and there is now here, and indeed, throughout the Caribbean, a great new wave of concern amongst the clergy that the Church should play an active part in the life of the various territories and, in particular, on behalf of those who suffer. Although there is still, and properly, absolute clarity about the necessity to keep the Church out of party politics, there is a growing recognition, particularly on the part of the younger clergy, that Christian concern must be with man's condition upon earth as an aspect of divine purpose as well as with the metaphysical questions of the life hereafter. Clearly, increasing inspiration is derived from the miracles of healing and the symbolism of the feeding of the multitudes as examples of Christ's concern for the sufferers and the disinherited.

If we are to understand the role that the Church may play we must remind ourselves of the central dilemma which party democracy creates for a developing nation. We defined this as being the problem of national and communal division which is a danger, if not a consequence, of a strongly entrenched party system at a time when the nation needs unity if it is to be capable of great achievement. In the Jamaican situation this problem is all too real. The two major political parties of Jamaica, the People's National Party and the Jamaica Labour Party, are both deeply entrenched in the life of the society and possessed of a hard core of support of fanatical loyalty. This loyalty partakes of an almost tribal character and has the effect of creating deep schisms within the society. For example, it is often difficult to get the members of a Jamaican village to unite behind a project in community self-help. At some point authorship of the project is attributed to either party, and most probably the party in power, which immediately divides the community about the desirability of the project itself. In fact, the more fanatical supporters of the party which did not originate the idea will probably regard it as a high point of duty to oppose, if not to sabotage the project. Thus, as we discussed earlier, the party political system has the capacity to paralyze communal will and poses the constant threat that all of the efforts which should reflect the national capacity for self-help are reduced to impotence.

In a situation where one of our problems derives from the tendency of the politics of freedom to create division, and in a country where the clergy is influential, there is a tremendous part which the Church can play. But first the Church must resolve its own philosophical problems and come to understand that the 'twin swords' of Aquinas may be separate but inhabit the same universe. Once the Church can understand that Church and State must, of necessity, be tangential although their ultimate focus is separate, the way is cleared for a unique contribution to a strategy of transformation. It must be safe to assume that the Church accepts equality and justice as the social expressions of the fatherhood of God. One must also assume that they accept Christ's ministry as embracing temporal concern. Upon these foundations one can construct the contribution.

In a situation where every politician is to some extent compromised by his party affiliation, the one man who stands out nationally and within each community as above and beyond politics is the clergyman. Further, the man in this position has a natural platform and with easy, one might almost say occupational, access to the people at large. It is he who can teach the lesson of national unity and co-operation. His is a voice that can proclaim the distinction between the legitimate conflict of democratic politics and the over-riding requirements of the nation. He can teach the lesson of unity without being suspected of political manoeuvring. He can call upon the people to unite in projects of self-help regardless of political attachment; his is the leadership that can set examples by handling the pick-axe

and the shovel and the street-cleaning broom without being
accused of political histrionics.

THE TEACHING PROFESSION

Perhaps the best way to assess the teacher's role in a strategy of
change is to consider the implications for the educational system.
We could do little more than hint at what is involved in the
last chapter. Yet we discussed enough to give some indication of
the magnitude of the teacher's task. What is required is nothing
less than a total transformation of outlook and method. Teachers
must undergo a process of self-transformation: they must comprehend a new set of objectives; they must evolve a new set of
techniques that can give effect to new targets; and simultaneously
they must keep the actual system running. Fortunately, we are
singularly well served in our teaching profession in Jamaica which
has a strong leadership content that not only understands the
new challenges of education but has often been in the forefront
of the clamour for change.

The highest priority must attach to these developments and to
the teaching profession itself. A teacher, literally, must carry the
whole brunt of the battle to create a new generation with a
different value system. Their's is the task to inspire future generations of children with positive attitudes towards work, social
responsibility and co-operation. Their's is the task of devising the
techniques which will make the young child learn to enjoy the
experience of production on the land. They must, somehow,
plan the group activities that lead to the creation of the spirit of
communal co-operation. And all this must be accomplished in the
face of a contrary parental influence in the home. It is going to
call for remarkable insight, dedication and application. Probably
the success or failure of the attempt at transformation will, in
large measure, be determined by the extent to which the teaching
profession can be inspired to a fanatical zeal for the kinds of
change we have been discussing. This implies, in part, a complete
re-thinking of the status of the teaching profession in society.
Teaching must become attractive to the finest minds in the
society because only the finest are likely to evolve the techniques
that are needed. The profession, therefore, must not only be
attractive in the scale of professional remuneration but must be

prestigious in the sense that the primacy of its role in the
strategy of change is understood and recognized by all.

THE COMMODITY ASSOCIATIONS

Since change in a democracy can only be accomplished through
consensus it follows that all the institutions of the society must
be mobilized to contribute to the process. But the mobilization
must be voluntary and must, therefore, depend upon communication which in turn begins with the admission and recognition of
the special place in the society of the particular body. The
commodity and producers' associations, the voluntary associations
and the professions are all highly developed in Jamaica. These
bodies possess institutional form and awareness of a common set
of interests which, taken together, create clear group self-
identification. The Chamber of Commerce, the Jamaica Manufacturers' Association, the Institute of Directors, the Jamaica
Employers' Federation, the National Farmers' Union, the
Jamaica Agricultural Society, the All-Island Cane Farmers'
Association, the All-Island Banana Growers' Association, the
Nurses' Association, the Bar Association, the Civil Service
Association, the Jamaica Medical Association, the Society of
Chartered Accountants and many others, all share, in varying
degrees, these qualities of institutional identity and are therefore
all capable of contributing either negatively or positively to the
process of change in accordance with their degree of mobilization.

Since these groups all exist for the explicit purpose of pro-
moting group interests, they are all likely, left to themselves, to
view change in terms of the needs of those interests. As a result,
there is often a substantial conflict between change as conceived
by a group and a strategy of change for a society as a whole in
the terms in which we discuss it in this book. However, it would
be an error to assume that this conflict cannot be mitigated or
even that it must always necessarily exist. It may well be that
there is often the occasion for conflict and where this clearly
exists, there must be the political will to ensure the primacy of
the national interest. However much unnecessary conflict is
caused and tension bred because of a failure consciously to build
bridges of understanding between a government committed to

change and the institutional groups which form part of the society to be transformed. In the absence of such understanding the possibility of conflict is maximised and, further, the consequences of conflict escalated. For example, the members of a group may be upset by a particular piece of legislation which promotes the national interest at their own expense. A bridge of understanding at this point may mean the difference between a quiet, if unhappy, acceptance of the new state of affairs and an active campaign of hostility which may lead to actual sabotage. This can be specifically illustrated. A government may feel it necessary to introduce a measure of control over the operations of a profession. Where there is dialogue, the profession may actually assist in designing the method of control and persuade its members to go along. In the absence of dialogue the professional body and its members may not only oppose the identical measure, but stage a professional strike or go-slow in protest. The difference between these two responses may be the difference in the method of approach. Hence, although the politics of change demand iron will on the part of leadership, its effectiveness is enormously enhanced by human understanding. It is this human element which must be recognized in a democracy; and it is the finest quality of democracy that it demands this understanding of those who wield power. This recognition of the human element in the atmosphere of freedom lies at the heart of the politics of participation.

THE VOLUNTARY ASSOCIATIONS

Jamaica has a great tradition of voluntary service. It may well be that this reflected nothing more than a twinge of conscience on the part of the privileged at the spectacle of a society so unjustly ordered. Whatever the motivation, it is a tradition of intrinsic value and one which can be organized and mobilized to great effect in a strategy of change. In the presence of such a tradition, for example, the appeal for volunteers to man a national literacy campaign has an instinctively receptive audience because it is a part of the tradition of the society to respond.

Where resources are limited and the tasks immense, no society in search of justice through democratic means can afford to ignore the voluntary spirit. Furthermore, this spirit is not only of value as a factor which can be mobilized to work for change, but is, in itself, a creative avenue through which men and women can express their instinct for service. When the more and the less privileged of the society come together on a project like literacy or work together to provide an infant school which may be temporarily beyond the resources of government, they educate each other in the dynamics of social unity. The less privileged may benefit from the skills and more highly developed sense of order of their better placed brothers and sisters, but equally, the more fortunate can learn much about courage, endurance and the quality of humour in adversity from the 'sufferers'. Both learn in a way that words cannot teach what it is to be part of the same nation as equals. Indeed they may well be taking their first course in equality.

THE PROFESSIONS

At a more technical level the professions can make an indispensable contribution to change and development and are the more likely to make it if there is a feeling of involvement in the thinking and planning that is taking place in the society. We have already considered at some length the importance of technical adaptation and the development of a relevant technology. The professions have a vital part to play in this process. By training and situation they are strategically located in a number of areas of the society. They possess, therefore, an unrivalled, practical knowledge of the workings of the institutions with which they deal and of how these institutions relate to the needs of people at large. For these reasons, the professional can point the way to practical innovation having the knowledge both to explore new and original paths and to ensure the avoidance of unnecessary mistakes. Nor can we afford to overlook the importance of professional innovation.

One of the mistakes that is made by many developing societies stem from the attempt to short-circuit history and apply professional expertise to the needs of people in the precise form which it takes in more developed societies. This often imposes severe limits on the rate at which professional services can be provided since one is of necessity seeking to apply them in their most advanced and probably most expensive, metropolitan form. A perfect illustration of this can be provided by considering two possible approaches to the development of medical services. It can be assumed that medical attention must be provided only by highly trained doctors and nurses in nothing except the most perfectly equipped hospitals or clinics. This will ensure a fine, but extremely limited service because it is a very costly enterprise.

On the other hand, one can take a realistic look at the kinds of medical attention that people do in fact require and can deliberately build into the professional medical services, a para-medical element which operates at the lower end of the services normally provided by doctors and, again, at the lower end of the services provided by nurses. In this way, nurses can be trained to take over a large part of the work-load of doctors thereby releasing the latter to a more widely available concentration on the more technical reaches of their own expertise. Simultaneously, the development of nurses' aides can release the fully trained nurses in exactly the same way and can, furthermore, be used to bring simple medical help right into the home thus reducing the capital cost involved in building clinics within reasonable distance of every household. A nurses' aide who is trained at relatively low cost to deal with the patient in the home is bringing some of the elements of consolation to the hard-pressed housewife which in a more affluent situation she seeks in her personal relationship with a family doctor.

The second method, involving a substantial para-medical element, represents original innovation in response to the practical realities of the economic situation of a developing country and can completely revolutionize the relationship between the medical service as a whole and the people. For this to work, however, there must be a declaration of independence from metropolitan norms on the part of those who govern accompanied by a communication of purpose to the professional body concerned. Where this is present, both can combine to bring elements of a just society to the people at large in response to clearly felt needs.

THE CIVIL SERVICE

There is probably no institution which finds it more difficult to come to terms with the politics of change and the dynamics of a participatory democracy than the Civil Service. Nor is there any single institution which makes a more critical contribution to the success or failure of the enterprise. This is so for two main reasons. In the first place, the Civil Service throughout the democratic world is in the throes of fundamental change of its own, in response to the changing role that is required of it by modern government. Originally, and certainly up to the end of the nineteenth century, government activity was regulatory in the main. It was the business of government to see that law and order were maintained, that accurate weights and measures were applied to produce and that a framework of general predictability was provided in the country at large so that those whose business it was to produce goods and services, could do so in an atmosphere of certainty. It was not the business of government to intervene actively in the productive sector nor to be the main agent in the provision of services. Hence, the civil servant's role was that of a regulator. It was his business to administer the rules by which the society governed itself and to give effect to the laws by which the law-makers modified the rules from time to time.

In the twentieth century, however, government has emerged more and more as the main creative agent in the economy. More and more, government is involved positively in production or in determining the policies by which producers must be guided. It is involved as the main provider of services and as the stand-by agent to secure action wherever the economy flags. This has required, as a general proposition of modern government, a major transformation in the role of the civil servant. From being an administrator of prohibitions, he is now required to be the creative promoter of schemes. The civil servant has become, therefore, the main manager of the society with all this implies for the creative, productive function as distinct from the negative, regulatory one. Developed, metropolitan societies have found it difficult to achieve the degree of transformation within the Civil Service that this change in circumstance demands. In developing societies where the government must of necessity play an even more dynamic role than would be the case in a metropolitan country and where there is a less developed Civil Service to begin with, the problem is both more urgent and more difficult.

The second main cause of difficulty lies in the peculiar role of the Civil Service in a colonial situation. In an independent nation in the nineteenth century, the regulations which were imposed upon society by government were at least the expression of the will of that society as expressed by its own system of power. In a colony regulations were the expression of an alien authority and were often repressive to an extent that reflected the relationship between the ruler and the ruled. In addition, these rules were enforced with all the arrogance which was the natural characteristic of the ruler. Consequently, colonial Civil Services added to all the limitations of their world-wide counterparts, an indifference to the people at large which was the unconscious reflection of the colonial equation. Thus, the Civil Service in a post-colonial situation faces not only the challenge of technical adaptation but also of attitudinal transformation. It must learn creative management and it must also learn to feel involved in and concerned about the need for change.

All of this requires, of course, the massive re-training of the Civil Service. This is partly a technical exercise but means also, the clearest responsibility to devise a method of training that has a strong philosophical content. Effective and rapid change will only be possible where there is a Civil Service with the managerial skills to give effect to the politician's reach for change and where there is a universal enthusiasm for the creation, through the opportunity of freedom, of a just and viable society.

THE MACHINERY OF GOVERNMENT

The machinery of government must, as a matter of common sense, be kept under constant review. Like all machines it is capable of improvement and adaptation and functions better in differing circumstances in accordance with man's capacity to make adjustment to its structure and operational methods. The Jamaican Government is no exception and is now in the process of considerable technical adaptation as it adjusts to the new challenges of independence. The need for new planning institutions and methods is becoming apparent along with the exploration of techniques of inter-ministerial collaboration and cooperation. An earlier chapter drew attention to the importance of a complete restructuring of local government. Detailed examination of these technical questions is, however, inappropriate in a conceptual exercise. There is a general problem, however, which has a considerable bearing on the role of government in the politics of participation and the administration of rapid change. This involves the capacity of government to harness the skills and talents that exist outside the bureaucracy.

No developing country can hope to overtake its priorities in a strategy of change with the bureaucracy that it inherits from colonialism nor with the kind of bureaucracy that it can hope to evolve in the short-run of independence. The government process must, therefore, consciously seek to enlist the best minds in the private sector of the economy, the universities and the professions. The problem, however, lies in the difficulty of harnessing these talents to the administrative process itself. Many difficulties present themselves. The bureaucracy is resentful of the 'outsider' and is quick to assume that the outside presence represents a lack of confidence in existing administrative resources. The newcomers, on the other hand, are impatient of Civil Service procedures, sometimes with good cause, and sometimes because of the failure to recognize the special requirements of public accountability along with the delicate balances that exist within a political system. As a consequence, Jamaica has tended increasingly to rely upon the device of the statutory board which seems to by-pass the problems on both sides of the fence by creating a semi-autonomous area of government, outside the scope of the Civil Service and its constraints, yet tied to the political process by the device of ministerial responsibility. This has had the effect in Jamaica of fragmenting the government service unnecessarily and has led to a huge network of statutory boards which often do not work in a co-ordinated fashion and are difficult to make responsive to a central concept of government. A happier solution to the problem lies in the use of consultants within the governmental machinery. By this means external expertise can be brought into the government process at the consultant level or as personal advisers to the Ministers who exercise political control. The price of personal friction which attends upon this method is more easily paid than that which is involved in the creation of an irrational, unwieldly and increasingly unmanageable network of statutory boards.

Another example of the difficulties which are faced in harnessing the skills of the society arises, once again, from the uncritical transplanting of the Westminster model. The Jamaican Constitution provides for a bicameral legislature; the Upper House consists of a majority appointed by the Prime Minister and a minority appointed by the Leader of the Opposition. The Constitution goes on to provide that the Cabinet which is made up of the Ministers who hold the various government portfolios and whose membership is drawn in the main from the lower, elected House of Representatives, may contain only three Ministers who are appointed from the Upper House. This places an unnecessary constraint upon the ability of a government to draw upon the widest reservoir of committed talent in forming the main components of a government of change.

The theoretical justification of the view which limits ministerial appointments to those who have come through the direct process of elections may be justified in British circumstances. In Jamaican circumstances these considerations must have a lower priority to the requirements of expert management in the search for development and change. Where the party system underwrites the probability of loyalty to proclaimed objectives, and where the political party has submitted itself to the elective process, it is an idle imposition to limit the search for ministerial talent to those who have actually faced the electorate themselves. In fact, it can be argued very strongly that it is the people who suffer when a substantial proportion of those who stood for election are obliged to devote the overwhelming proportion of their time to ministerial duties. Ministerial duties can only be performed at the expense of constituency representation and, hence, the maintenance of communication between the people and the government. There should be balance in all things and Jamaican Government would be most effectively organized if more attention were paid to constituency representation and popular communication on the one hand, and if it were possible to maintain a higher average level of executive ability in the composition of the Cabinet. In a small country this is not easy because there is an inevitable limitation upon the number of seats in the elected assembly (in Jamaica's case the constitutional limit is sixty) yet the ministerial functions of government are considerable. In fact, the complexity and specialization of government does not decrease proportionately with small nations in comparison with large ones. Hence, it is a mistake to assume that the human resources available to a government in Jamaica and to be drawn from a total Parliament of sixty members is equivalent to those available to a British Government with a Parliament of more than six hundred members. A constitutional amendment giving greater freedom in ministerial appointments would make for greater flexibility and efficiency.

Any strategy of change must of necessity involve sacrifices on the part of various sections of a society from time to time. Man accepts sacrifice when he has a sense of commitment to the outcome of a process. A critical element in the politics of change, therefore, is faith. This implies not only an acceptance that the goals and methods that are being employed are moral and sound but also that there should be faith in the leadership which proclaims the goals, defines the methods and calls for the sacrifice. It may be that old societies have evolved a general public acceptance of public morality. This, however, is not necessarily true of societies that have come recently to the experience of modern political institutions. Bearing in mind that justice needs the support of appearance, it is not difficult to see that faith in public integrity must rest upon manifest fact. In politics, objective fact, illusion, appearance are all inextricably bound up in the question of whether leadership can in fact lead because it commands credibility. For this reason, and particularly because development in the democratic context rests exclusively upon the enthusiastic participation of the people at large, it is vital that the political leadership be of unimpeachable and manifest integrity. This, in turn, implies the wisdom of taking steps to secure that integrity be made as manifest as human ingenuity can devise. To this end it is highly desirable that a system requiring the declaration of incomes and assets be established by law. Obviously, we cannot legislate for honesty. On the other hand, we can provide the machinery through which suspected dishonesty can be investigated and, equally importantly, can proclaim through law the principles by which we intend to be guided. It is particularly in this sense of the declaration of intention that this type of legislation is invaluable for the development and maintenance of the level of public confidence which is indispensable to the enterprise of change.

THE PRESS

No strategy of change can be developed without considering the role of the press. This, in turn, involves the comprehension of what the term 'press' implies in today's world along with a critical analysis of its role in a free society.

In an earlier age the idea of the press involved anything from gossipy news sheets to the tracts through which men like Jonathan Swift attacked the corruption and ineptitude of the leadership of their times or the savage social commentary of a Charles Dickens. Always, however, one was dealing with the written word which to be effective as an instrument of communication implied a literate reader willing to buy the paper, tract or journal and who was prepared to devote the time and concentration to reading the material. However persuasive the arguments presented in the journalism of yesterday, the nature of the exercise guaranteed that the exchange would involve a quality of consideration on the part of the reader. To the extent that the reader had to make an effort one could assume the possibility of some degree of intellectual resistance to the worst reaches of propaganda.

Modern technology has completely transformed the relationship between the communicator and the public. In addition to the written word which is now churned out with a speed, frequency and a skill in packaging completely beyond the reach of yesterday's journalism, there has been added the whole range of communication through the electronic media. This has meant that the average citizen is exposed to an almost limitless range of techniques through which he can be brainwashed. For those who may have thought George Orwell's *Nineteen Eighty-Four*[1] the exaggeration of a counsel of despair, I would suggest a quick reading of the most chilling book to have emerged from the democratic milieu, *The Selling of the President*.[2] This book has done for our comprehension of the political process what *Hidden Persuaders*[3] did for our insight into modern marketing. *The Selling of the President* lays bare the anatomy of the political

[1]*Nineteen Eighty-Four,* George Orwell, Secker & Warburg, London, 1949.
[2]*The Selling of the President,* Joe McGinniss, André Deutsch, London, 1970.
[3]*Hidden Persuaders,* Vance Packard, Longman, London, 1957.

campaign which took a candidate and an electorate, analyzed the latter and packaged the former so that he seemed to represent the answer to the deepest and often basest fears of the average voter. Implicit in this exercise was the total cynicism with which the people, the candidate and any philosophy about the society which both inhabited was regarded. No one is so naïve as to suggest that any communication which seeks to persuade can be devoid of propaganda. However, modern technology has put at the disposal of the communicator a battery of techniques which has created an entirely new dimension in society and poses dangers of a new form of totalitarianism by consent which Orwell foresaw with startling clarity.

Clearly then, man now has at his disposal instruments of enormous power for good or evil in the field of ideas and access to the processes by which opinions and attitudes are formed. This armament may be put to the purposes of tyranny as was the case in Orwell's particular vision. Equally, they can be put to constructive use in the reshaping and revitalizing of attitudes. Certainly, no political process predicated upon change can disregard the significance of the communication media in this wider sense.

It is important at this point to distinguish carefully between the use which is made of the communication media by those who wield power in the political process; and the question of the press itself as an element within the political process itself. Because of the very totalitarian dangers which Orwell foresaw, the question of legitimacy in relation to the use of the media by governments and political parties is extremely sensitive. It is possible, however, to distinguish certain areas of principle and practice which make the analysis of legitimacy more manageable. For example, we can agree that governments should not use their power to secure the use of the media in the exclusive interest of the political party upon which the government itself rests. The self-restraint that is involved in this distinction may be difficult to practise but is necessary for the preservation of the democratic process since the slightest invasion of this principle will lead inevitably to the totalitarian management of the media for the purposes of maintaining power. On the other hand, it is the duty of a government to enlist the full range of media technique in the support of policies and as an instrument in the development of the new attitudes which may be necessary for the success of the policies themselves. Once this distinction is understood and maintained, the integrity of the democratic process is preserved while the vitality of the strategies of change are enhanced.

It is always far more difficult to agree on the proper role of the press in a free society. Indeed, there are even those who contend that there is no 'proper' role for the press because the very idea of a predetermined role contradicts the concept of freedom. 'Freedom of the press' represents one of the institutional responses to tyranny which emerged from the eighteenth and nineteenth centuries and which taken together, provided the broad framework for what has come to be termed the free society. Indeed, the phrase has become for the professional journalist what Magna Carta is for the private citizen. Both, however, emerged in a time when the right to one's liberty was a dominant consideration in the pursuit of justice. But these rights are not ends in themselves but only elements in the total fabric of justice. We accept that there cannot be a just society if that society does not provide a defined area within which there is freedom of action and predictability of status for both individuals and institutions. Equally, however, we must recognize that there is no justice in society without the recognition by individuals and institutions of their responsibilities to the whole. Thus, the concept of 'freedom of the press' which conceivably appeared to involve an absolute objective in the beginning and which is still a predominant consideration in totalitarian situations, is still subject to the entire question of social responsibility. Increasingly, this must be a matter for concern in free societies which are grappling with the problems of change in the search for social justice.

The laws of libel and decency have long since made the freedom of the press subject to certain defined rights of the individual. Equally, the press is going to have to recognize that its freedom is subject to an over-riding concept of general social responsibility. And it is precisely here that the difficulty arises. Where is the dividing line between the rights of the press to its freedom as one of the main instruments by which a free society protects itself against totalitarian encroachments, and the claims of social responsibility?

G

Because this line is so difficult to draw; because it is so difficult to decide what is an over-riding social responsibility to which the press should be subject, it is to be hoped that the issue never has to be decided by a government acting unilaterally in restraint of the press. On the other hand, the press itself must recognize that if it will not impose restraints upon itself through self-discipline, it invites a confrontation sooner or later. The press cannot expect an institutional licence that puts it beyond the scope of the authority of society itself. For example, the press cannot expect its freedom to be defined to include the right to lie and to distort merely, for example, because it may disagree with a policy being pursued by a duly elected government. There are other ways in which honest disagreement can be expressed and provided the disagreement is expressed honestly the press is entitled to its freedom.

What is needed, and earnestly to be hoped for, is a constant re-evaluation by the press of its own role and responsibilities. Critical to this exercise is the recognition that its freedom is earned to the extent of its recognition of a concomitant responsibility. This is the critical intellectual decision which, once taken, will make confrontation not only unnecessary but impossible in a political system which is committed to the principles of a free society. In the final analysis the press should interpret a society to itself through the accurate presentation of news and by creating the avenues through which all the significant currents of opinion in the society can find expression. In short, the press should seek to educate and inform.

It should also be the role of the press, through the social concern of crusading journalism, to illuminate the hidden corners of misery and neglect in a society. Just as the press is a bastion of liberty so too should it be a repository of the nation's conscience. It should be alert to corruption and quick to uncover suffering and always on guard to challenge a society to excellence. All this can be accomplished within the context of the present organization of the press provided there is a common and fundamental acceptance of the principle that an onus of responsibility rests upon the institution itself. Once this challenge is accepted, the press can be a critical agent in the processes of change. If the decision is not taken, however, the press can be a destructive and regressive force. If the latter course is chosen, sooner or later confrontation between the press and the forces of political change becomes inevitable. Where the confrontation takes place, freedom is the casualty. Therefore, to those whose commitment to freedom implies a desire for change as to those whose search for change is pursued in the name of freedom, it is vital that the press remain free and accept the duty of responsibility as the price of that freedom.

WOMEN

No discussion of an egalitarian society would be complete without consideration of the special position of women. Equality is indivisible. But in many societies women are not equal. Jamaica is no exception. Jamaican women do not have full equality before the law in a number of respects and particularly in marriage. More often than not they get less pay than men for the same work. They do not enjoy equal job opportunities and often suffer while substantial public and unemployment relief works are designed with men exclusively in view. There are only two women members in an elected Parliament of fifty-three, only one woman member of a Cabinet of nineteen, no women ambassadors and no women in top Civil Service posts. All this happens in spite of the fact that girls have equal access to early education and have a generally superior record of academic performance. It happens, too, in spite of the fact that women have been the backbone of the Jamaican family for a century and tend to be just as active in the political system. Clearly, therefore, the disabilities from which they suffer in adult life are the products of systematic discrimination reflecting deep-seated prejudices in the society. There is nothing in all this that is peculiar to Jamaica whose women would certainly enjoy a superior status to that obtaining in many developing countries. It is, nonetheless, an intolerable invasion of the principle of equality.

Social justice and commonsense alike dictate the need for a systematic programme of legislation and institutional modification to the end that women take their full and equal part as dynamic and involved participants in society and contributors to the processes of change. Laws must be revised to remove all traces of discrimination, training programmes must be devised and job opportunities scrutinized to ensure full equality of opportunity. Economic development must be planned with the needs of women in the employment area fully in mind. In this way one will simultaneously satisfy the principle of equality and release to the use and benefit of the society, the enormous reservoir of energy and talent that is locked away in the female half of the population. Jamaica must work consciously towards a situation in which women play a full part in every aspect of national life, bringing to bear their equivalent general abilities together with the special qualities of commonsense and patience which they seem to acquire as part of the preparation for and experience of motherhood. In any event, it is impossible to conceive of social justice unless the decision-making process at every level of activity in the society reflects the female equally with the male viewpoint. Each sex views reality from the perspective of its particular role in the family relationship. Each, therefore, complements the other and policy proceeds most wisely where it represents a resolution of forces as between the male and the female perspectives.

MINORITIES

Minority groups, in ethnic and religious terms, have been well treated historically in Jamaica. There has evolved a substantially tolerant tradition and hence, minority relationships do not represent a major problem in the island's development. One must, nevertheless, pause to insist that discrimination in any form is the antithesis of social justice. Indeed, the treatment of minorities by the majority is one of the testing grounds of the depth of acceptance of the notion of social equality. Clearly, there is a dual responsibility in this regard. Minority groups owe it to society to identify totally with the nation of their adoption and its aspirations. Those which retain a dominant attachment to the lands from which they spring, are an irritant within society that begs for the irritable response. Therefore, the first duty of a minority group is to ensure that the primary attachment is to the land of citizenship rather than of origin. This does not by any means imply the abandonment of the original culture. Rather, it implies that the original culture must be seen in its historical perspective and kept in contemporary context. The historical culture must not be allowed to obtrude upon the society though it may always complement it. Equally, the 'host' majority is mature to the extent that it accepts the diversity which the minority groups bring to the total culture as long as this is clearly in the context of a general willingness to be a part of the nation as a whole. Provided this diversity is in a clear context of their acceptance that they are a part of the nation, the minority group is entitled to its full and equal place in society. Indeed, the extent of which a society is able to accept its minorities is a measure of its maturity.

YOUTH

We now turn to that critical but elusive category, youth. Today's youth are capable of making either the most dynamic contribution to change or of impeding it through senseless disorder. In Jamaica, as elsewhere, the mood of dissatisfaction amongst the young tends towards an unprecedented intensity. This tempts a repressive reaction on the part of the establishment. However, the intending architects of a new social order cannot afford the luxury of inter-generational squabbling. Nor is it prudent to ignore the younger generation which is always the source from which a society can hope to draw the advance guard of its collective conscience.

Youth is best understood taking into consideration two factors. First, there is the effect upon young minds of the values which they find in the society which surrounds them. Second, there is the effect upon a young person of the educational system during the preparation for adult life. Experience is the process by which a human being evolves from the uncomprehending confidence of the baby through the discovery of danger to an accommodation which reflects increasing knowledge about the environment, its control and the processes by which danger may be contained. All of life seems to involve the cycle of innocent hope succeeded by disillusionment but leading, eventually, to a more cautious optimism founded upon knowledge.

Adolescence is the birthplace of idealism. To the young person, ideals are tangible things from which the best of life's expectations are hung. A moral idea, to a young person, represents a categorical imperative requiring a positive human response in the arena of action. Thus, adult action is judged by the young in relation to proclaimed ideals. This is in sharp contrast to adult evaluations of the same conduct. The adult will judge action in terms of an assessment of pragmatic necessity. He may regret the extent to which this necessity occasions departures from the ideal but he is unlikely to allow the ideal to determine his actions. To the young person, to whom an ideal is a command to action, adult behaviour patterns appear as a form of chronic betrayal. Thus, throughout history wherever young people have been exposed to ideals through education, religion and parental instruction, they have tended to respond with that single-minded intensity that is their special quality. Consequently, the older generation has been viewed with disenchantment if not contempt. This problem has grown more acute with time. Education in the modern world is available to an ever increasing proportion of the young. Simultaneously, this age proclaims its ideals as vociferously as any other and a lot more audibly since modern communications have multiplied message and audience alike every time the philosopher, the politician or the preacher opens his mouth.

Accordingly, the younger generation in the second half of the twentieth century views life from the perspective of a far more sophisticated appreciation of moral, political and social values than its peers of yesterday. Simultaneously, it is more aware than ever before of the ideals which society proclaims for itself. Finally, the modern communication system ensures that every failure of human conduct in the light of proclaimed ideals is brought to the immediate attention of the entire population. This chronic, patent contradiction between precept and performances lies at the root of the most dangerous component of the 'generation gap'.

Much of adult intolerance of the young stems from a guilty conscience. In the main, the young may be hasty and inexperienced; but basically they are right. The answer, therefore, to the disillusionment of the young is not to be sought in their reform but instead, in the reform of society. Rather than dismiss the young as intemperate or, at best, naïve society would do better to enlist the younger generation in the struggle to build a better world. For the real answer to the scepticism of the young is to be found in their involvement.

Young idealism represents one of the great untapped resources of modern society. The young can be enlisted in literacy campaigns and to till new soil; they can be enlisted in the taking of a census of the handicapped and they can help man the schools which lack instructors. What the young need most of all is to feel involved in the processes by which they can help to make their own ideals come true in their society. Hence, a National Youth Service, to which reference was made in another context, is not only important to ensure the development of the egalitarian idea and as a means of increasing the productive capacity of the society at large. It can also represent a critical avenue through which the young may express their own commitment to social idealism.

In an entirely different context, the world is witnessing a growing confrontation between the younger generation and the establishment about the place of the former in the decision-making process. To the unthinking members of the older generation, youth is a time for obedience. The moment when the young person may be admitted to the decision-making process is a time to be postponed as long as possible in this adult view. On the other hand, the young have always pressed for a voice in affairs at the family, institutional and national levels. In recent history, however, the pressure has grown more acute as its justification has increased. This is entirely due to the pressures of modern life. We live in the technological age and endure an explosion of knowledge without parallel in history. Human survival has always rested upon knowledge. But the acquisition of knowledge in today's world is a completely different phenomenon compared with the experience of a mere generation ago. The average youth preparing for the General Certificate of Education O-levels today is likely to be far better educated than his or her parent. To this must be added the fact that the world is both more competitive and more uncertain for today's young. The educational process by which a child is prepared for the job market of a modern economy is increasingly competitive. The average child experiences pressures in this regard that were quite unknown to earlier generations. As a consequence, young people feel that the adult world places demands upon them of which they are acutely conscious and with which they must live but which they cannot influence. All this takes place in the context of homes that are either broken or fractured or are the scenes of a chronic discord which does little to engender respect for adult ways.

The logical response to the pressures of the modern world upon the young is a mounting frustration at society's persistent and stubborn denial of their presence in the decision-making process. Obviously, all adjustments to the methodology of a society must be subject to the constraints of common sense. It would be idle to canvass the case for unlimited participation by the young in the decision-making processes of the society at large. Common sense dictates a realistic adaptation in response to new circumstances. The case for the vote at eighteen is unanswerable and the case for simultaneous majority legal status is probably sound. Political parties and institutions generally should create avenues through which the young can contribute and participate wherever possible. The whole society can only benefit by this process. To the extent that they are involved in the responsibility for decision-making, the young are prepared for the realities of adult life. Even more so is this vital in a free society seeking to mobilize through participation. The younger the exposure to decision-making the better the preparation for the management of the institutions of a free society.

The most important area in which the young claim the right of participation is in education itself. Many educators are reluctant to permit the genuine involvement of students in decision-making. The issue is obscured by the contention that the young cannot decide what they are to be taught since, by definition, that is precisely what they go to school to learn. At best the right to some form of general student council is admitted in this view. If, however, education is a preparation for full membership in a particular society, it must prepare for that society in the fullest sense. A free society depends upon the capacity of every citizen to bear responsibility by understanding the demands that responsibility makes upon understanding and discipline alike. Therefore, education must prepare the young for responsibility which suggests, in turn, that students should grow accustomed to taking a responsible part in the management of their own affairs. The debate should not be as to whether students should have a voice in the management of students affairs and extra curricula activities; nor whether they should have a voice in the choice of courses. Rather, the adventure should be the discovery of how to make a dialogue between teachers and students a creative part of the educational process itself. With the young as with all other elements of society, participation is the best guarantee of performance and harmony alike.

6

First Directions

I AM writing the final chapter of this book after some fifteen months in office. The party that I have the honour to lead, the People's National Party, was returned to power after a ten year absence with a sweeping mandate for change. We polled more than 56 per cent of the popular vote in the elections of 29th February, 1972. This was a remarkable result in a country whose politics are rooted in a deeply entrenched party system and where, for example, our traditional opponents, the Jamaica Labour Party had won the elections of 1962 and 1967 with slightly under 51 per cent of the popular vote on both occasions. The size of our 1972 success stemmed partly from superb political organization, partly from an imaginative campaign but far more importantly from popular discontent. I have tried, by implication, in this book to analyze some of the causes of this discontent and equally I have sought to suggest a strategy for change and to anticipate some of the political difficulties that confront those who are committed to change within the framework of Western style democracy.

The last fifteen months have afforded me ample opportunity to put my ideas into practice and to observe both popular and institutional reaction to the process. The wind of change is blowing strongly. It is like a presence in the political atmosphere and as its implications are sensed by the masses – that is, the workers, the small farmers struggling with marginal hillside land, the poor mothers in the slums, the youngsters and even the children – there is a stirring of popular excitement and anticipation, a renewal of faith, a light in the eye of the disinherited who sense that their claim to a place in the national life is a dominant consideration in governmental and political action. And where expectation is high, the problem is one of management so as to secure that hope, newly rekindled, will be sustained by performance. Simultaneously, there is a restless, inchoate fear amongst the more privileged members of the society who feel threatened by change. Here, the problem is one of reassurance: how to make the better-off members of society realize that the progress of the poor is not at their expense but, rather, a condition to be desired in natural justice and the goal that all must seek if social stability is to be preserved. It is a time of high feeling in which both expectations and fears are inevitably exaggerated since the hope of the masses is born of the depths of their despair and reflects the degree of their historical deprivation. Equally, the fears of the privileged are born of the apparent challenge to their economic and social status and reflect their present inability to discern their role in a refashioned society.

Looking back over the first fifteen months it is fascinating to consider the main steps that we have taken and which together have created this charged atmosphere. They fall into seven main categories and each represents no more than a first and belated essay in a policy aimed at a just and self-reliant society. The fact that they have had such emotional and psychological impact indicates the chasm which separates a post-colonial society from a system of social justice however loosely defined.

Within the first year of office we mounted the psychological assault on three main fronts. Jamaica's Labour Day has always been celebrated on 23rd May, the anniversary of the worker uprisings in 1938 which separate the Jamaica of post-1865 from our more modern history. The tradition had developed of treating Labour Day as an occasion for political rhetoric backed by shows of force in which the two major political parties strove to out-do each other as repositories of popular faith and expectation. The exercise had become increasingly violent in the arena of rhetoric no less than that of demonstration, and an air of unreality had begun to envelop the occasion.

We decided to make a dramatic break with the past and called upon all the people to come out on Labour Day to give a day of free work to their nation on some project of social utility. In 1972, tens of thousands of persons poured out to plant trees, start beautification projects, repair old peoples' homes or lay the foundations for basic schools. Four hundred and ninety-four projects were actually identified as having been started and subsequently brought to completion as a result of that day. Its impact upon the community was dramatic. It was clear that a new dimension had been introduced into our national life and that a great feeling of love, unity and purpose suffused the society. As a consequence, the self-help movement received tremendous impetus and hundreds of projects, mainly in the area of infant schools, community centres and sports grounds, have been launched since Labour Day 1972. By 1973, of course, the Opposition Labour Party had regrouped its forces sufficiently to declare itself unalterably opposed to the idea of working for the community on Labour Day. They have made it a test of party loyalty not to participate with the result that the 1973 exercise had less of the quality of national unity and joy. The number of projects actually commenced on Labour Day had just about doubled from 1972 and generally speaking were much better organized and purposeful. Much more of concrete value was accomplished; but a primary purpose of the day, which is to create a sense of national purpose going beyond class and political party divisions, has been substantially blunted by the opposition's 'dog-in-the-manager' stance. Nonetheless, the self-help movement proceeds apace and the net gain to the society is substantial.

At the same time we have tackled the problem of freedom of dress by introducing an alternative acceptable form in the 'kareba'. This caused a considerable flutter amongst the members of the establishment and has become an additional point of controversy since the opposition Jamaica Labour Party have emerged as firm champions of the traditional European jacket and tie.

Throughout this period I have appeared all over the island to take part in work projects along with my Ministers, Members of Parliament and other members of the administration. Arriving informally in our 'karebas' we have chopped trees, cleared bush, gathered stones, forked land; I have even tried my hand at chipping at a huge cotton tree which was being fashioned into a fishing canoe. The intention is to teach the idea of social unity, community of purpose and the dignity of labour. This is in sharp contrast to the traditional view of elitist participation in work projects which consisted on the one hand of a wifely cutting of ribbons and, on the other, of a patently over-clad gentleman making a half-hearted pass at the terrain with a pickaxe. The fact that the earth was only marginally disturbed by

these efforts seems to have worried no one. Nor did the fact that
these ceremonies served only to underline the gulf between ruler
and ruled seem to cause undue concern. However, I am happy
to say, for the benefit of those who believe in the traditional
method, that the Opposition Party remains firmly committed to
this view of establishment participation.

Faced with considerable balance of trade problems and a huge
food import bill while thousands of acres lie idle, we have
launched a massive attempt to feed ourselves which we called
Operation GROW. In the first six months of this effort more
than seven thousand acres of idle land either held by government
or acquired from private ownership have been brought into intensive food cultivation. By the end of 1974 we hope to have
brought some twenty-five thousand acres into production in what
will be the first really concerted effort to achieve a measure of
self-sufficiency in food. These projects are launched with popular
work days in which thousands of citizens volunteer a day's work
clearing the land. These days have been a tremendous success
and have witnessed men and women, rich and poor, Custos, the
Reverend Man of God, Minister of Government and cane cutter
working side by side forking the land and clearing stones. A late
lunch is shared by all followed by a meeting in which we ex-
pound the philosophy behind the effort. All who have shared this
experience come away enriched by the rediscovery of their common humanity and the joy of sharing a day of common purpose
in which it is the purpose that is the reward.

These food farms are operated as government projects in the
first instance. However, when they are well established in terms
of management, crop methods, working arrangements and
marketing, we intend to turn them into co-operatives in the
ownership of workers of proven reliability and efficiency. These
worker-farmer co-operatives will then work in close collaboration
with the Government but will, hopefully, form viable economic
units actually owned by the people who have built them up by
discipline and hard work.

A parallel operation to the food farm project is called Project
Land Lease. Under this effort we persuade land owners who
have not the means to put all of their own land into production
to lease the surplus to government. We in turn distribute this
land on a lease basis to deserving farmers of proven capability

suffering from a shortage of arable land. In the first three months of this programme more than 1,000 farmers have received additional parcels of good land in close proximity to their existing, inadequate holdings. These farmers are encouraged to produce crops of proven marketability and strong marketing services are being developed for them.

These are but two early aspects of a programme which envisages the substantial restructuring of the agricultural sector – a sector whose value to the Jamaican economy is critical. Unfortunately, while much lip service has been paid to the question of revitalizing the industry, little has been accomplished in the way of practical programmes.

At present, a team of advisers headed by one of the Caribbean's most eminent economists, Sir Arthur Lewis, is engaged in an Agricultural Sector Study which is expected to yield much of value to guide the Government's agricultural planners in the next few years.

In other areas, strenuous efforts are being made to rationalize production of our traditional crops such as sugar and bananas.

I remain unshaken in my belief that we will not begin to solve our economic problems until we create a strong, viable agricultural sector which will satisfy a large percentage of our local food requirements, as well as achieve competitive levels of productivity and provide an economic base upon which to rest a revitalized rural life. Here, too, we must explore those new and more democratic systems of ownership of large units of land by the men who make them produce, a policy to which we are committed.

One of the great problems in the development of poor countries like Jamaica arises in the field of nutrition. The unrestricted operation of a free enterprise system coming out of a colonial background tends to exclude from its benefits substantial sections of the population. As a consequence, malnutrition is surprisingly widespread in spite of the apparent paradox that this represents in an agricultural country. The imperatives of social justice and economic development combine to insist on the importance of a well-fed population with an adequate protein content in the diet. Faced with this problem, we have decided to move the government into the field of nutrition and are establishing our own nutrition complex. We have just formed a government company called Jamaica Nutrition Holdings Ltd through which we intend to operate a number of ventures. The nucleus of this operation is a school feeding programme which will supply a fortified school children's milk and lunch pack. The initial plant will have a daily output of 110,000 units and it is our intention to expand this as rapidly as resources allow.

At the same time we have taken over the responsibility for certain key imports such as wheat, soya, corn, rice, salt-fish and similar products that are critical inputs into the low-cost mass diet. We have entered into partnership with the local flour mill so as to ensure adequate supplies of cheap flour which we can subsidize if necessary as a low-cost carrier for high protein soya mixtures and cereals. We intend to develop our own milling capacity in relation to soya beans and are also experimenting with soya planting on our food farms. We intend to develop the complex so that it can take rejected, surplus bananas for the development of our own banana cereals. We are also experimenting with cassava as a source of the starch based flocculent which our huge alumina industry uses in the process by which bauxite is converted into alumina. Through this nutrition and milling complex, working in partnership with private enterprise at some points but providing our own milling capacity at others, we intend to pursue the objective of an adequate, high-content, low-cost diet to the population (and particularly the children) along with industrial and agricultural linkages in which we tie our own agricultural development to our objectives in nutritional and other fields. Once again this has led to strong popular approval coupled with considerable apprehension among the leadership of the private sector.

Perhaps our biggest effort in the first year has been in the field of the development of human resources. We have launched our massive literacy campaign which is aimed at eliminating functional illiteracy in four years. We have established the foundations of a free educational system at the primary, secondary and university levels. This system removes all educational costs from the private citizen and establishes a clear system of merit for the movement from primary to secondary academic, secondary technical and, finally, university education. Simultaneously we have been able to add a further two years for half of the primary system which involves education to the age of seventeen instead of the age of fifteen which was standard for the whole primary system one year ago. As soon as resources allow we intend to extend the whole primary system to the age of seventeen. Simultaneously, we will, by next year have doubled the annual intake of the secondary and technical systems and will in due course tackle the capacity of the university at one end of the scale and the problem of infant education at the other. It is interesting to note that infant education has been the principal beneficiary of the self-help movement where wonders have been accomplished in terms of infant school plant and volunteer teachers.

The literacy programme has benefited from the voluntary spirit as well; some 12,000 volunteer teachers are now operating in the field. Our industrial and agricultural skill training programmes which are centred mainly in workshops run by our Ministry of Labour and Employment and youth camps run by our Ministry of Youth and Community Development, will have more than trebled their combined capacity at the end of the first two years of this government.

An interesting comparison which serves to illustrate the size of the effort which we are making in the field of education and human development emerges from the following figures. Each age group in the Jamaican population now consists of around 50,000 children. For example, there are 50,000 fifteen year olds in the island at this time. One year ago only 8,000 out of those 50,000 in each age group received any kind of education or training whatsoever beyond the age of fifteen. The remaining 42,000 left the primary schools with no hope of any further training with which to prepare themselves for the demands of a modern economy. At the end of our first two years in government, we will have increased the number of children receiving education beyond the age of fifteen from the present figure of 8,000 to 32,000. By the end of our first term of office we will have taken this development even further and will be able to guarantee an education up to the age of seventeen for every single boy and girl born in the country.

Allied to all this we have commenced a system of National Service in which we will be requiring all those who benefit from the free secondary education system up to the 'O' level examination standard, that is to say, up to the age of seventeen, to give

two years of National Service to the country. They will be free
to volunteer to work in any of a number of government fields
and will be well looked after in terms of board and lodging,
pocket money and the like. During their period of National
Service they will be free to qualify themselves for further education in the event that they had been unsuccessful at any point.
The two year service stint can be given either at the end of the
'O' level period of education when they are seventeen, or at the
end of the 'A' level when they are nineteen, or at the end of
university provided it is given at one of those points. In this way
we hope to recycle our higher skills into the process of national
development while imbuing the concept and spirit of service and
social unity. I see this exercise in both pragmatic and conceptual
terms. Pragmatically, it will prove an important element in the
effort at skill-mobilization in development. Conceptually, I regard it as critical to the development of the psychology of
an egalitarian society. This programme is consciously aimed
at the reduction of that tendency among those who enter the
elite through training to extend the elitism of their skill to a
psychology of exclusivity. It is critical to the development of a
concept of social justice that elitist skill should carry with it the
instinctive acceptance of enlarged social responsibility. Only thus
may the egalitarian spirit survive and transcend the divisiveness
that is inherent in differences of personal attainment. Inevitably,
the introduction of free secondary education and national service
have led to a certain alarm among those who were accustomed
to rely upon their wealth as the guarantee of educational opportunity for their offspring. Similarly, there is 'upper class' unease
about National Service.

These tremors of concern have not been calmed by the fact
that taxation policy has reflected the new social dynamic. For
the first time, we have introduced substantial increases in
property taxes and in a form that is designed to tax wealth.
Agricultural land in substantial production has been specially
exempted but property generally has been made the subject of
rapidly escalating rates based on a uniform system of unim-
proved value. The intention is explicit and deliberate. It is, on
the one hand, to make those who can afford it, bear their fair
share of the cost of development. On the other hand, it is designed to put pressure on the holders of idle land to either put

that land into production or to dispose of it to others who are willing so to do.

In the field of law and citizens rights, we have abolished a system of mandatory sentences for minor offences which had seriously invaded judicial discretion in the area of punishment. Simultaneously, we have established the equality of women in the area of citizenship as it bears on the rights of non-citizen spouses. Previously the non-citizen wives of male citizens were accorded rights denied to non-citizen husbands of female citizens. Equal pay for equal work now obtains in all government employment. And we have ended centuries of legal discrimination against illegitimate children.

We are concerned that public, and particularly parliamentary life should be as honest as we can contrive to make it and determined that we make a visible effort to secure this end. Accordingly, we have enacted legislation requiring all Parliamentarians to declare their income and assets annually to a Parliamentary Commission. The declaration is confidential in normal circumstances, but the Commission has wide investigatory powers and irregularities established *prima facie* are subject to possible prosecution in the Courts of Law. The maximum scale of penalities provided is heavy, including prison terms. This measure has provoked an interesting philosophical debate but I stand firm in my conviction that the claims of the public good are paramount and must take precedence over the right to privacy of the citizen where one has offered oneself for public service.

Finally, there have been exciting new initiatives in the field of foreign policy. Within the first year, we have moved from an unadventurous and relatively closed foreign policy to an open one. While retaining our traditional friendships in the West and, indeed strengthening those considerably, we have made it clear that Jamaica regards herself as a part of the world and that we have no interest in the power struggles with which the major metropolitan powers divert and excite themselves. Like all developing countries we need to be the recipients of foreign capital and technology and we seek these wherever we can find them on terms compatible with our national interests. We have made it clear that we feel free to trade where we can find the best bargains and have sent missions to explore new trading possibilities around the world. We have made it clear that we regard the Third World as a group who share a common economic history and face a common economic dilemma. We are exerting our influence to focus the attention of Third World nations on the economic realities of their situation and call constantly for the avoidance of ideological distraction among the members of the group. We are consciously seeking avenues of trade as between Third World countries in the view that every item exchanged between Third World countries reduces the dependence of the group upon traditional trading patterns with the metropolitan world. This exercise is of vital importance in our minds because of our experience of the constantly adverse movement in the terms of trade between developing and metropolitan countries. We are planning to organize and host a Third World economic conference in 1974 aimed specifically at the establishment of a Third World development fund and the institutions through which the exchange of Third World technology can be encouraged and avenues of Third World trade explored.

In the Caribbean we have played a decisive part in moving the region forward from the original free trade area, CARIFTA, which was established in 1968, to the establishment of a Caribbean Community and Common Market which was launched by Jamaica, Trinidad and Tobago, Guyana and Barbados at Chaguaramas, Port of Spain on 4th July, 1973. The Agreement, which arose out of what is known as the Georgetown Accord arrived at in Guyana earlier in 1973, represents a historic step forward in the regional economic movement. We are satisfied that economic regionalism is an important element in any strategy of Third World economic development and is particularly important in the Caribbean where the unit nations are too small to provide the market base upon which substantial economic development can rest.

In all of this: the new approach and strategy of Labour Day; the new emphasis upon self-help; the symbolism of freedom of dress; the massive government effort to grow food; the careful government strategy in relation to nutrition; the huge mobilization of resources in the fields of education, literacy and youth development; totally new dimensions introduced by National Service; the challenge to traditional patterns of law as they relate to crime and punishment, women's rights and illegitimacy;

the essay in wealth taxes represented by the property tax and the outward-looking policies in relation to the Third World and the Caribbean; the emphasis has been on the conscious remodelling of society in terms of social justice, self-reliance and equality. The people at large are already beginning to realize that change has a form and a purpose. It is becoming clear that the winds of change blow in a predictable direction because they come from a past whose deficiencies have been analyzed and they tend in a direction whose virtues we seek consciously to promote.

Some of the establishment anxiety in the face of all this has been trivial both as to its cause and in its extent. For example, reaction to freedom of dress has been mild and many members of the establishment are already beginning to enjoy the greater comforts of the new style. Reaction to Labour Day, self-help and the great work days which launch the new food farms has been widespread and enthusiastic and reflecting all the hallmarks of a popular mobilization that catches up rich and poor in its good nature and constructive excitement.

Similarly, reaction to the literacy programme has been extremely favourable at all levels as also that which greeted the new initiatives in the fields of law, women's rights and the like.

The four areas of clear confrontation are those involving taxation, National Service, government activity in the economy and foreign policy.

Insofar as taxation policy is concerned, it is inevitable that those who have more will object to being taxed more. This is a completely predictable and normal human reaction which clearly will not last. Nobody likes paying taxes but in the end everybody comes back to the grudging recognition that it is a necessary part of the functioning of government within organized society. In so far as National Service is concerned, the objection runs deeper and the resistance will doubtless be more sustained. At root, the National Service system challenges the unconscious, separatist assumptions of an elitist society. These are not advantages to be lightly surrendered. On the other hand, if we are serious about a society of equality, it is a confrontation that must be faced and overcome because success at this level is completely fundamental to the concept of society that one is seeking to fashion. The truth is, the upper class resistance to the idea of National Service is emotional and irrational. Their children will benefit enormously from the practical experience gathered during two years working with the government; economic development will benefit enormously through the harnessing of their skills; and the society will benefit from the fact that advantaged and disadvantaged will combine for national purposes without regard to divisions of status and training. In any event, all the young people in National Service, whether they come from the poor homes whose children will now enjoy higher education, or the better-off homes whose children will continue to enjoy higher education, will be well looked after and will, in the main, be giving their service from the base of their own homes since it is not intended to have a military dimension to the period of National Service.

There is perhaps no aspect of the new policies which is provoking greater hostility to less purpose than government participation in the economy. The protagonists of the free enterprise system have always invested their activities with a mystique that owes little to reality but a lot to the attempt to elevate the notion of free enterprise into a theology. In fact, all societies devise for themselves various methods by which they accomplish their objectives. The Pharaohs of Egypt and the sugar planters of Jamaica once used slave labour. Other societies at other times have tilled the soil on the basis of a family unit while other families produced master craftsmen in gold assisted by a small number of personal retainers. Jamaica, in common with the great majority of the nations of the world, operates a mixed economy. By this we mean that the government on behalf of the people organizes a certain number of the activities which the society must undertake while leaving it to private individuals to do the rest. This has always been so and will doubtless, continue to be so. From time to time the country enlarges or contracts the number of activities which the government is to undertake with a consequent contraction or enlargement of those that are undertaken privately. From time immemorial, even those activities that are undertaken privately are undertaken within a careful framework of laws which regulate, on behalf of the public at large, the extent to which the private undertaking is free to act as it pleases.

Basically, the kind of economy that we are attempting to construct involves the following principles. The government is undertaking the development of human resources, and the provision of infrastructure on its own. This involves the educational system, substantial proportions of the medical services, the roads, the water supplies, the public utilities and the like. It also involves the field of basic, low-cost nutrition because nutrition is an essential element in the successful development of human resources. In so far as the economy is concerned, the government identifies certain priority areas the development of which is strategic to the capacity of the rest of the economy to perform. This obviously includes light and power and industries such as cement which is a vital element in low cost housing and in future road construction. Where an area has been identified as strategic, we consider whether the private sector is both willing to attempt and capable of achieving the development without which other parts of the economy cannot function. Where we are satisfied that it is willing and able we are content merely to supervise its effort so as to ensure that this is effective and consistent with the national interest. For example, we could not sit by and see a monopoly in a strategic industry either refuse to expand at the rate that was needed, or to insist upon levels of profit which were unreasonable and created prices that the economy could not afford.

In other cases the government will enter into a partnership with private enterprise so as to ensure compatibility of the particular economic activity with the national interest or because the private sector may be unable to raise finance on the scale that is required. In yet other cases we will operate on our own as a government either because the private sector cannot attempt the job or because it would be unfair to ask the private sector to do so having regard to the special national needs in the particular case. For example, recognizing nutrition as a critical element in human resource development, if we decide that certain items of food must be made available at very low cost, it may be impossible for the private sector to make profits at the prices which are involved. In this event the government has got to undertake the enterprise possibly even involving an element of subsidy if the national objective is to be achieved. It will be observed that all of these decisions flow from a pragmatic evaluation of society's needs and are no more ideological in their orientation than the decision, which Jamaica took many years ago, to make education a field primarily for government rather than private sector effort. What is critical to the whole pragmatic exercise is to keep two things clearly in mind. On the one hand, private enterprise works in terms of certain operating laws. Essentially it involves the investment of money at risk for the purpose of supplying the answer to something that people want in return for the making of a profit. Arguments, therefore, about the legitimacy of profit in the private enterprise system are as irrelevant as arguments about whether we have the right to breathe. Breathing is as necessary to our survival as are profits to the operation of the private sector. Debate about both is idle. Equally, however, we have to remember that private enterprize is a methodology, not a right. The private enterprise system is a way of accomplishing social objectives. It is not a theological right divinely ordained and therefore beyond control in the name of social responsibility. Nor does it imply an unlimited licence to operate in every aspect of social and economic activity. Much of the recent hysteria in Jamaica, and in a limited circle there has been considerable hysteria, has stemmed from a petulant misunderstanding both of society and of the role of the private sector itself. Our view is quite simply that once certain priorities have been overtaken in the field of human resources, infrastructure and certain strategic areas of the economy private enterprise is the method best suited to the production of all the other goods and services which are necessary to the functioning of an economy. Once these definitions are grasped with intelligence and maturity, the dichotomy between the private and public sector is seen to be unreal. Both are merely parts of the whole, both are subject to the overriding requirement of social responsibility and both are essentially complementary to each other and are often required by circumstance to operate in a manner that overlaps. In due course the institutional leadership which has traditionally spoken for the private sector will come to learn that the expansion of the public sector which is taking place at the moment will greatly enhance the capacity of the private sector to perform by improving the context within which it seeks to do so. When better trained and better fed people with a stronger sense of responsibility to their nation come forward to man the factories, productivity will have its best chance of rising. But this will only happen if the leadership in the private sector makes a similiar effort to drag itself into the twentieth century. If the leadership of this section of the community spends its whole time with its eyes riveted on the past and oblivious to the great changes in attitudes and performance which it needs to attempt in its own ranks, it will suffer the fate of all people similarly preoccupied. On the other hand, there is a chance now for the whole nation to rally to new challenges and new opportunities. Equally, the masses must understand their own responsibilities to see education as a challenge to effort and not some casual passport to an easy life. Families must begin to be planned by parents who suddenly realize that a new world is taking shape in which opportunity will go to ability and within which the skill rather than the numbers of a family will determine the place that it occupies in the society.

Finally, in the field of foreign policy misplaced theologies about international relations have done much to obscure reality. Jamaica has suffered from an establishment view of the world which approximately equates the notions of international conspiracy which were current in the days of John Foster Dulles and the notorious Senator Joe McCarthy. The fact that the world has come a long way since then has passed largely unnoticed in many quarters of Jamaica. However, for every older establishment personality who has found a certain security in the belief that Jamaica is a little outpost of empire whose independence was to be regretted and at all costs contained by being accompanied by no visible change of policy, there are thousands of young people who need to feel part of a larger national adventure. Today's young are impatient of the limited horizons of yesterday's philosophies. They observe detente between Germany and points east all the way to Russia and between America and points west all the way to China. With their formative years spent in the decade of independence, today's younger generation realizes that international relations represent the new arena of opportunity and that our external dialogue does not condition our internal polity.

The fears of some members of the older generation of an open foreign policy reflect the acute insecurity of a people fashioned in the colonial trauma. If one's formative years were spent under the shadow of an imperial authority it is an instinctive part of one's assumptions that any external relations involve the importation of somebody else's ideas and somebody else's systems.

On the other hand, it is of the essence of freedom that one can develop the confidence to know that we fashion our internal political system for ourselves; and from the posture of that confident certainty seek our relationships in the outside world to our national advantage within a context of a sense of general international responsibility.

As we embark upon this adventure one comes to recognize how much in politics rests upon both common sense and compassion, how much rests upon a clarity of vision and purpose, and how much rests, finally, upon sheer will.

It takes great common sense to know that the hopes which are released by the early promise of the politics of change must be justified by subsequent performance. Equally, it takes great common sense to know that the private sector has a vital part to play in that performance and must be given the confidence to make the contribution of which it is capable. It takes great compassion to understand the past pain to which new policies seem to hold the answer and to determine that the causes of that pain must be removed in tomorrow's social order. Equally, it takes great compassion to understand the fears of a man who has worked hard for what he has, who has a lot and now fears that he might lose it. He must be made to understand that our mission is creative and not destructive and that we wish others to experience his sense of accomplishment by opening the doors of opportunity and not by pushing him back down into the obscurity from which he has climbed.

It takes great clarity of vision and constancy of purpose to hold to policies in the face of the articulate opposition through which small but vocal groups try to divert us from our purpose. And finally, in the small hours of the night when uncertainty and the consciousness of human frailty tend to creep up on their unsuspecting victims, it takes a will of iron to hold to your course and to know that you are summoned by fate to common sense, to compassion and to unswerving purpose. If the moral purpose of this mission is to remain intact, it must be approached in humility and supported by prayer. Hegel once remarked that 'history is the march of God in the world'. Ours, then, is the task to see that the road tends ever towards justice.

Index

Acton, John Emerich Dalberg, Lord, 56
advertising, 157
Africa: independence of, 124; and Jamaican heritage, 20, 28, 147–8, 154–5; liberation movements in, 131; political system in, 25–6, 28
Agricultural Sector Study, 206
agriculture, 19, 86; and exports, 79–80, 81, 97, 99; and food farms, 205, 207, 212; future of, 91, 96–100, 120–2, 205–7; lack of growth in, 89–90, 96–7; and land ownership, 205–6; wages in, 89–90, 173; *and see* hill farmers
All-Island Banana Growers' Association, 182
All-Island Cane Farmers' Association, 182
alumina industry, 88, 115–16, 119, 207, *and see* bauxite industry
aluminium industry, 132, 133
Anancy, 69
Angola, 130
arts, Jamaican, 85, 146, 148, 155–7
Aswan Dam, 106
Australia, 132, 133–4

Bahamas, the, 127
banana trade, 79, 97
banking system, 86, 104, 118–19
bankruptcy, 59
Baptist Church, 29, 178
Bar Association, 182

Barbados, 127, 211
bauxite industry, 19, 83, 115–16, 123, 132; in Australia, 133–4; foreign control of, 86, 104; future of, 91, 102–3, 118–19, 207; statistics on, 102n; wages in, 86, 89, 173
beaches, 19, 109
Belize, 126–7
Bermuda, 127
Bevan, Aneurin, 104
Bogle, Paul, 178
Brazil, 127
British Council, 148
Bustamante, Alexander, 21

Canada, 123–4, 125, 129
Capitalism, 17; and economy, 109–12; *laissez-faire,* 35, 59
Caribbean, the, 20; role of Church in, 179; role of in Third World, 124, 126–7, 135, 136, 211
Caribbean Common Market, 126, 211
CARIFTA, 211
Castro, Fidel, 106, 158
Chamber of Commerce, 163, 182
character, Jamaican, 27–9, 30, 48–9, 135–6
Church, the, 30; Baptist, 29, 178; and social change, 178–81
Civil Service, 80, 141, 188; and social change, 185–7; women in, 195
Civil Service Association, 182
class divisions in Jamaica, 41, 45,

219